Math 7v7

Shawn Branson.

GOD'S STORIES

More Than Twenty Years on the Mission Field

SHARYN BRANSON

WESTBOW
PRESS®
A DIVISION OF THOMAS NELSON
& ZONDERVAN

Scriptures taken from the Holy Bible, New International Version®, NIV®.
Copyright © 1973, 1978, 1984, 2011 by Biblica, Inc.™ Used by permission
of Zondervan. All rights reserved worldwide. www.zondervan.com The
"NIV" and "New International Version" are trademarks registered in
the United States Patent and Trademark Office by Biblica, Inc.™

WestBow Press books may be ordered through booksellers or by contacting:

WestBow Press
A Division of Thomas Nelson & Zondervan
1663 Liberty Drive
Bloomington, IN 47403
www.westbowpress.com
1 (866) 928-1240

Because of the dynamic nature of the Internet, any web addresses or
links contained in this book may have changed since publication and
may no longer be valid. The views expressed in this work are solely those
of the author and do not necessarily reflect the views of the publisher,
and the publisher hereby disclaims any responsibility for them.

Any people depicted in stock imagery provided by Thinkstock are models,
and such images are being used for illustrative purposes only.
Certain stock imagery © Thinkstock.

ISBN: 978-1-5127-7279-1 (sc)
ISBN: 978-1-5127-7280-7 (hc)
ISBN: 978-1-5127-7278-4 (e)

Library of Congress Control Number: 2017900925

Print information available on the last page.

WestBow Press rev. date: 07/25/2017

Dedication

This book is dedicated first and foremost to God who saved my life and continues to be my Daddy!!! Secondly, this book is dedicated to my husband, Paul, who loves me and has encouraged me for years to write this book and my children, Noah and Samantha of whom, together with Paul, make my life complete and full of happiness. Also to our foster daughter, Anny, who has brought much joy into our lives.

I lift my eyes to the hills. From where does my help come from? My help comes from the Lord, who made heaven and earth.

Psalm 121:1 & 2

Mission: a journey with a purpose

Missionary: characteristic of a person
engaged in a religious mission,
as defined in the "Canadian Oxford Dictionary"

Missionary: a person engaged in sharing
the love of God and Word of God with
others so that they can take a step closer
to God. *as defined by Paul & Sharyn*

Foreword

By Rev. Dr. Keith Attles

In this amazing account of the true missionary experience by Sharyn Branson, she beautifully paints a vivid picture of a faith-building journey involving the will of God and foreign missions. Every sentence is filled with the hope and faith needed to accomplish such a daring task for the Lord from Canada to the Dominican Republic. Both Sharyn and her husband Paul's obedience to the call of missions will greatly inspire you to endure any and all challenges you may face with love and grace.

This book is a wonderful account of the many events and circumstances Sharyn's family overcame in order to fulfill the Lord's will. Within these pages you will read about financial miracles, accounts of salvation, powerful stories of God's healing grace and answers to prayer, as they were delivered time and time again. Faithfulness to the calling is what authentic ministry is all about and your heart will be inspired as you read through the many experiences in this book.

Two of my favorite stories in the book are the story about the $4000.00 offering they received as an answer to prayer to pay for plane tickets to the mission field, and the other about their adoption of Noah after realizing that they could never have children on their own. Both stories are infused with an absolute confidence in the Lord's ability to bless beyond measure as one remains steadfast and faithful to Him in all things. My hope is that you too will be inspired to believe that God is able to do all things if we simply trust and have faith.

Preface

My husband, Paul, and I have been in foreign missions since 1995. We have been blessed to experience over and over again God's many blessings and see Him move mountains for many people, including ourselves. This book is a collection of God's stories that God has allowed me to be a part of. My prayer is that by putting these stories on paper, that first and foremost, God will be glorified, and secondly, that reading these true stories, written from my perspective, will encourage and inspire you, the reader, to grow closer to our Heavenly Daddy. God wants each one of us to be living for Him who created us and loves us more than anyone else possibly can.

Acknowledgement

I thank God for the life that He has chosen for me. I get up every day excited and loving what God has called me to do. I never went looking for a life like I have had but I am so blessed to have served God, using talents and skills that He has given me, to serve Him in a manner that He wants me to.

I want to thank my friend, Kim, who encouraged me and proof read this book for me. I struggled on the order and she was the one who gave me the idea to put this book together as excerpts from a journal.

I thank each and every person who has supported in one way or another so that we can be career, full time faith missionaries, serving God as He has called us to. You have supported us in so many ways from finances to mission teams, to items donated, to your sweat and labour, to allowing us to share in your congregation, and most importantly, your priceless prayers.

Thank you to my family. Paul, Noah and Samantha. God and you are my reason to life. You bring me more joy every day than words can every express. Your support of my desire to write this book has been beyond words. Thank you for loving me.

"For I know the plans I have for you, declares the Lord, plans for welfare and not for evil, to give you a future and a hope."

Jeremiah 29:11

Introduction

In 1995, we found ourselves on the Mercy Ship, M/V Anastasis without a clue as to what we had signed up for. After completing a five month Discipleship Training School, we returned home to Canada to inform our church and family that we were going to go overseas and serve our God in full time, career faith supported missions. Some thought that we were nuts. Others were very supportive. Then, when God sent us to the Dominican Republic, Paul told God that he was signing on the "two year program". Now we joke and say that we are just waiting for the two years to start.

I have always enjoyed writing poems and little stories. This book is a collection of various experiences that we have been blessed to be a part of during our more than over twenty years in full time, foreign missions. My prayer is that this collection of stories will inspire, encourage and bring people closer to God in a new way that they have not experienced before.

I have come to experience that in today's church, many believe that God does not still do miracles like we read about in the Bible. In this book, you will read about God miraculously healing people, providing for people, feeding people and more. You will read about God being God… A Daddy who loves and cares for His children and who wants to touch the heart of every human being because we….. YOU are His child, too.

1994/1995

We had been married only three years and like so many other young couples, trying to figure out what to do in life and where God wanted us. We had heard about a ministry called Mercy Ships that sails around Europe and Africa doing various types of ministry work while sharing the Gospel. On the ship, they also offered a five-month mission training school called "Discipleship Training School" or DTS for short. After some prayer, we decided to apply to this school. We were accepted but we needed about $15,000 to cover all of our expenses. This money would pay airfare, school fees, and necessary pocket money needed for five months.

We started to share with our church and friends about the DTS and to raise funds to go. We could not go to the ship until we had all the funds in hand. Our church was very supportive of us but it was a small church of about twenty families. We knew that we would have to find other means to raise the funds needed. We sent out letters, shared with everyone who would listen and prayed a lot.

During this time, we continued to work, attend church, bible studies and live as before. The date came and went for the DTS that we wanted to attend. We could not attend because we did not have the funds. Another school would start in six months so we worked towards being able to attend that school. The deadline for the first 50% of the school fees was quickly approaching and we did not have the funds. We were both really feeling that God did not want us to do this DTS; or any DTS and that maybe we were not to go into missionary work. One night, we prayed that God would "write it in the sky" if He wanted us to go into missions and take this DTS school.

Two nights later, Paul was at a friend's home where they had a small Bible study with Paul and the couple of the house. The three of them had been having a weekly Bible study for about a year and had grown close. On this night, Paul went to the Bible study and the couple started the evening by saying that they wanted to talk to Paul. They proceeded to tell Paul that they felt that God was telling them do something and it involved Paul and I. They said that they were planning to make a large purchase of a luxury item but God had stopped them and told them to give the money to us instead. They asked Paul how much money we needed to go to the DTS. Paul said that we needed $15,000. This couple did not know before this moment how much money we needed. When Paul said the amount, the couple looked at each and then laughed. Paul had no idea what was going on. Then, the husband reached into his breast pocket and pulled out a cheque that he had written that afternoon. It was made payable to Paul and it was for exactly $15,000.

God wrote it in the sky!!!! The next was the deadline for getting the 50% of the school fees posted off to the school. Three months later, we left to meet up with the ship in London, England (which God also blessed us being able to celebrate our fourth anniversary in England two days before joining up with the ship.)

September 1995

We had been in Banbridge, Northern Ireland since the beginning of August to work with the YWAM ministry there. We were a team of fifteen from the DTS (Discipleship Training School) and this was our outreach time after completing a three-month theory part of the school. We would spend two months in Banbridge ministering with YWAM (Youth With a Mission). The YWAM ministry operated an alcohol free coffee shop. The coffee shop opened just before school let out in order to catch the after school crowd and stayed open until one hour after all the pubs and rave clubs closed. The purpose of the coffee shop was to ministry to the youth who came into the coffee through friendship evangelism in a comfortable atmosphere of a coffee shop. Our job was to serve drinks, prepare snack type food, be in constant prayer and reach out to socialize with those who came into the coffee shop.

Through the coffee shop, we met a young man who quickly informed us that he use to be a Christian until the Christians showed who they were really were and he went running in the opposite direction. This young man, George, now hung out with another young man who was dressed all in black, always wore a scowl on his face and just looked creepy. One day, George and his friend came into the coffee shop. Paul and I sat down to speak with them as it was our turn. The other members of our team were doing their jobs, as well as praying over our conversation. George's friend just sat there, not saying a word and looking off into the distance as if he was not even listening. We were asking George more about his him and not focussing on whatever hurt him in the past when he was a Christian. George brought the conversation around to Christianity so we just went along. He told us how Christians are all false, they are liars and never keep their word. We tried to tell him that not all Christians are like that. I said that I would keep my word to him. George then proceeded to ask a series of "what if" questions to test me.

All of a sudden, George's friend turns to me with a very scary look on his face, gets about six inches from my face, and in a deep voice says, "He is dead. Stop talking about him!"

I said, "Stop talking about who - Jesus?"

"Do not say his name. He is dead! Only Satan has the power." he says. By this time, our noses are almost touching and he pulls at my hair a bit in his anger towards me and Jesus. Then he turns to the other people on our team and screams, "Stop talking to Him! He is dead". Then he gets up and leaves the coffee house.

As our time went on in Banbridge, George would come to the coffee shop almost daily to hang out and just chat with the different members of the group. We all grew to love George and we were all praying for him. As our time was nearing an end, George started to talk more about how Christians all lie and none of us would ever keep in touch with him. Addresses were exchanged with some members of the team and promises made. I also exchanged addresses and promised to write, even if George did not write me. When the day came for our team to leave Banbridge, George showed up and accompanied us to the airport. It was great that he saw us off but I also felt a sadness for him as I felt he was going to be lonely and his only "friend" was that creepy guy.

When we got home to Canada, I did write George. I made a point of writing him every few weeks. As the weeks, and then months passed, I continued to write but George did not write me back. This was in the time when internet was not a household tool and most people did not have a home computer, let alone smartphones, tablets, etc. Our letters were sent snail mail and took time to reach George. About six months after our return to Canada, I go to the mail box to retrieve our mail and there is a letter post marked from Northern Ireland. I quickly tear I open and out falls a ripped piece of paper that says.

"I bet you never thought that you would get a letter from me. I wanted to write you to say that you now have a new brother in Christ. You did not lie to me."

I was so happy that I almost cried. I could not believe what I was reading and had to read it again. Amazing - George had turned back to God. I could not wait to share this news with Paul. About four months later, George showed up in Canada for a two weeks visit. It was great to see him. He looked like a new man, glowing with the love of God in him. We had some great talks and great times. One of our friends who was on the DTS with us and in Banbridge lived close to us and became friends with George. She also kept her promise and wrote

George. The four of us had a great time during George's visit to Canada.

We have not seen George in person since his trip to Canada but we have kept in touch. Now that Facebook exists, we keep in touch on Facebook. George is now married, has children, plays in the church worship band and is a fine man of God. Praise God for all the work He has done in George's life.

"Trust in the Lord with all your heart and lean not on your own understanding, all your ways acknowledge him and he will make your paths straight."

Proverbs 3:5-6

November 1995 – June 1997

How Did We End Up in the Dominican Republic?

How did you know where to go? Why the Dominican Republic? How did you become missionaries?

These are questions that we have been asked an uncountable amount of times since we became career faith missionaries so it seems a fitting way to start this book.

After completing a Discipleship Training School (DTS) with Youth With a Mission, we had returned to Victoria, BC, Canada from Northern Ireland and England. During our time in the DTS, we felt that God was calling us, as a couple, to do more in missions. We had no idea what this meant or what God wanted from us but we were willing. We had a return flight bought to Victoria so that is where we went. The first things on our list of items to do were to find jobs and talk with our Elders.

We both found jobs fairly quickly. I (Sharyn) returned to working with the Red Cross. They hired me on a contract basis to assist some directors, write programs and teach all levels of first aid courses. Paul found a job with small, one-man computer company that build PCs, sold and repaired PCs. We were thankful to have work and incomes.

Our church asked us to give a report to the Elders and Deacon,s as well as to the church congregation on our past six months of ministry overseas and doing the DTS. We were thrilled to do this. Our small church was such a huge support to us in every way imaginable. Their love, and prayers carried us through so much. The very least that we could do was to report back to them.

When we told our Elders that we felt that God was calling us to enter into full time missions and become faith living missionaries, they were incredibly supportive. We explained to them what we believed God had told us. God had not given us a heart for a specific people group. We felt God telling us to serve using the skills that He had given us. Paul with his construction skill and myself with my health education and medical skills. We desired to the return to Mercy Ships and serve them on one of their ships, principally, the M/V Anastasis. Our Elders were very supportive and asked what was required. Mercy Ships required that we have 90% of our monthly support raised before we could go and, we had to wait until a couple's cabin became available on the ship. At that time, there was none available. The Elders said that that was all fine and that they, as a church, would do all that they could help us to raise the support that we needed.

In the meantime, we would continue to work while raising our monthly support. Paul's parents generously allowed us to live in the small basement suite of their home, for very minimal rent. This was a huge financial blessing as we were then able to save more each month to put towards some of our one-time expenses like plane tickets to meet up with the ship. We started to prepare packages with all our information, mission goal, financial goal, etc and sent them out to churches and individuals to ask for their monthly support. This was a very slow process.

While working on raising support, we had the opportunity to go to Mercy Ships' United States base for me to take a ten-day medical mission's course which would help prepare me for medical missionary service. While at the base in Texas, Paul had appointments to meet with various people in regards to us joining the Anastasis. While meeting with various people at the base, they spoke with Paul about the idea of us joining the staff at the base in Texas while we waited for a cabin to become available on the Anastasis. They offered Paul a position in their base maintenance and myself a position in hospitality. At first, we did not like this idea; especially me because hospitality really is not an area that I have many skills in. However, we were both eager to start our missionary careers. We talked about this and started to pray about this while I finished the medical mission course and we returned to Canada.

As we prayed about the options available to us, with everyone's support and the elders' advice, the decision has to be made between God and us. We had to go down the path that we really believed God wanted us.

As the months dragged on, and one month turned into two, then six, then eight, then twelve, we were getting discouraged. We started to feel that we were wrong and we were to stay put in Victoria, serve at our church, continue in our jobs and schooling, buy a house and settled down. Paul had a friend who was a real estate agent and we started to look at townhouses and small houses - places that we could afford on our minimal incomes. Life started to fall into a "normal" routine for life for a young couple in Canada. Go to work five days a week, church on Sundays, Bible study on Tuesdays, hang with friends, etc. We started to get comfortable. Then God spoke very clear.

It was a typical Tuesday, like every Tuesday. I biked to my job at the Red Cross and Paul headed off in our car to his job at the PC store. Little did we know that this was the day that God was going grab our attention in a way that we could not ignore and our lives would never be the same again.

After being at work for about thirty minutes, the phone in my office rang. It was Paul. He said, "Can you get away for a coffee break? We have to talk." I responded by saying, "Yes, I can and yes we need to talk." Paul said that he would meet me at Red Cross and we could walk down to the coffee shop. About fifteen minutes later, Paul was there. We did not say much as we headed to the coffee shop and then Paul just pulled over.

"I do not have a job." Paul said.

"Neither do I", I said.

"What" we both said at the same time.

Paul went first. He explained that he showed up at the store and it was locked. He tried to call his boss and there was no answer. We found out later that for various reason, the store would never open again and Paul was left with job.

To preface my story a bit, you need the back story. This was in early 1997. The past few years had been very hard on the Canadian Red Cross due to the blood scandal where a few patients contracted Hepatitis B and HIV from blood transfusions with blood collected by the Red Cross. The court cases almost bankrupted the Canadian Red Cross. As a result, the Board of the Red Cross had held meeting on the night before (Monday) to make some drastic decisions in order to save the Canadian Red Cross. The main decision that they made was to change how the Red Cross was managed. Up until this point, the Red Cross had had eleven head offices across the country. In order to save money, the Board decided to divide the country up into four regions with only four head offices. This would cut a lot of staff and overhead costs of running only four head offices instead of eleven. As a result, many people who were hired on contract with the Canadian Red Cross had their contracts canceled at that meeting. On Tuesday morning, when I showed up for work at the Red Cross, I was informed that my contract was one of those many contracts that got cancelled the night before.

Just like, in less than an hour, both Paul and I were out of jobs! God was speaking very clearly and we were ready to listen. After two days of talking, praying and seeking God, we both came the conclusion that we were to sell all that we did not need, store what was necessary and pack up our car. Then, we would head east from Victoria, stopping along the way, to speak at churches and with individuals to raise up our monthly support to join Mercy Ships.

This was a totally crazy idea. We both knew it yet it still felt right to us. Our next idea was to go speak with the head Elder of our church. David was an older gentleman. I do not remember his exact age at this time but I think that it was around 80 years old. He had grown up with a very conservative Brethren background. I remember his grown daughter telling me how when she was growing up, they could not do housework, homework or even play a game on Sundays. We knew that we could not proceed to do anything without the consent of our church and our church officially commissioning us to the mission field. We decided that Paul would go talk to David. There was no way that David, conservative David, would consent to this crazy idea. We only had about 20% of our monthly support raised. There was no way that David would agree that selling all our possessions, packing up our car and to just start driving.

Paul called up David and asked if he could come to his home to meet with him. David agreed and invited Paul to come over the next evening. On Thursday evening, Paul headed over to David's. His lovely wife served them tea and left David and Paul to talk. Paul explained what had happened to both of us and losing our jobs on Tuesday morning. Paul also explained this crazy idea that we felt was from God. David sat back, drinking his tea and listening with his full attention as Paul explained all this and explained what we felt God was saying.

One thing that we all agreed on was that God was definitely trying to get our attention. By this time, it has been 18 months since we had returned from our DTS. We had gone from returning to the Anastasis, to serve in ministry through construction and health education/medical, to going to the base in Texas to serve behind the scenes in maintenance and hospitality.

David listened, asked a couple questions then just thought for a moment. Paul later told me that he was sure that his jaw hit the ground when David's next words were, "Paul, I believe that you and Sharyn are right. God is getting your attention and it is time to go!"

David was not supposed to say this. Conservative David was supposed to say "No, it is too risky. Look for new jobs. God will provide. Stay here until you have your support raised. The timing is not right." Instead, David spoke of how the timing is right, the time is here, we need to go.

Paul drove home in almost a daze and then it was my turn for my mouth to hit the floor as Paul told me about his meeting with David. WOW Could this be happening? Mercy Ships required us to have 90% of our monthly support raised before we crossed the Canada/US border. The plan would be to sell everything, pack up what we would need in our little Toyota Tercel and head east.

Our church was fully behind us. They commissioned us and threw a big party for us before we left. We were leaving knowing that we had so much love and prayers lifting us up on this journey ahead of us.

However, not everyone agreed. There was a couple that Paul had been doing a Bible Study with. Jack and Shirley are about ten years older than us, with two children. Ben called Paul and asked Paul to bring me to the next Bible study. Once we arrived, they sat us down and said that they really felt God laying it heavy on their hearts to share something with us. We thought that they wanted to sponsor us for our ministry work. We were so wrong. They proceeded to share with us that they have witnessed us go off to do the DTS and grow immensely. We returned to Victoria excited to answer the call that God had placed on our lives to enter a life of full time missionary service to God. They reminded us that when we returned from our DTS, we spoke so strongly of how God had not given us a people group, but rather the calling on the type of ministry He was calling us to. They shared how they had watched us start to go down one path and slowly veer off to another path until now, instead of serving on the front line doing construction and medical, we were headed to Texas to serve behind the scenes in maintenance and hospitality. Jack and Shirley spoke of how they have felt a heavy heart when they pray for us; that we are now on the wrong path and that they needed to speak up before we left. Being young and pig headed, we just nodded but inside were telling ourselves how wrong Jack and Shirley were.

We held a lot of respect for Jack and Shirley and valued their speaking into our lives, however, this time, we felt that they were just plain wrong. They must have sensed this. They then asked us to promise them on thing. They asked us to contact at least twenty-five other, front time, ministries and inquire about the possibility of us serving them in the areas of construction and medical. Due only to how much we respected Jack and Shirley, we promised to do this.

As we drove home, we spoke of how we disagreed to Jack and Shirley. We were not upset with them at all; they were just wrong and we were right. However, we had given our word to them to reach out to twenty-five other ministries and make inquiries. Over the next week or so, I researched and found email addresses for twenty-five locations. Now, remember, this was early 1997. The internet was not as big as it is today and many people, businesses, ministries and churches did not have web sites, let alone email addresses. I found the first twenty-five email addresses that I could. Then wrote a generic letter to send out. It was a short note. Basically, it introduced ourselves, said our basic skills, and asked if they had a need for a young couple with our skills. I then sent this letter off to the twenty-five email addresses that I had found. After completing this, we told Jack and Shirley that we had sent off inquiries to twenty-five locations, as promised. They were happy that we completed our promise and said that they praying for God's will to occur and, that if it is God's will for us not to go to Texas, that we would get a response from one of those twenty five notes.

We accepted the positions at the Mercy Ships' base in Texas, sold most of our possessions, said our byes and headed to the ferry to start our journey. What a scary and exciting moment this was. We boarded the ferry, went upstairs, and as we sat looking out over the Pacific Ocean as the ferry pulled away from the dock, we prayed that God would guide us every moment of the journey.

Our first stop was Langley, BC where we spent the night with Sharyn's aunt and uncle. It was great to see them and touch base with them before heading out on this journey. At this time, we had no idea when we would be back. The next day, we drove to Kelowna to visit Sharyn's grandparents for the night. Next, we headed to Alberta. Paul has a sister in Red Deer and Sharyn has a sister in Trochu. Sharyn's sister agreed to let us stay with them for a little bit while, as we reached out to local churches in Central Alberta for opportunities to share about our ministry that we were beginning on and, hopefully, raise more monthly financial support. Our plan was to stay with Sharyn's sister for two to three weeks.

Shortly after arriving in Alberta, we received on email back in response to the 25 emails that we had sent out. It was from YWAM in the Dominican Republic. They said that they had been praying for new staff, specially staff with construction and medical skills. Then, our email arrived and they felt it was an answer from God. They invited us to join the staff of YWAM in the Dominican Republic. Paul and I were so convinced that we were to return to the M/V Anastasis, that we promptly ignored this email from YWAM Dominican Republic.

We had put together some packages with information about ourselves, Mercy Ships and the ministry that felt God called us to. We mailed and hand delivered these packages to many churches in the Central Alberta area. The church that my sister attended allowed us to share and one other church in Innisfail also invited us to come share about our ministry. However, every other church that we contacted declined our request to share more about our ministry. As the days, then weeks passed by, we were starting to become discouraged. We talked, prayed and brain stormed as to what we can do next to raise more monthly financial support. All the while, my sister, her

17

husband and kids, put up with us sleeping on their sofa bed in their family room. As I look back at this time, I am so thankful to my sister and her husband and also wonder how they did not kick us out sooner. They were so graceful to put up with us for as long as we ended up staying with them.

About three and half months later, still staying at my sister's, Paul and I were very frustrated. We had no place to go and we had not had even one more person agree to join our ministry and monthly support team. What was God doing? What were we doing wrong? We finally opened our eyes enough to realize that maybe we were doing something wrong. Paul and I decided that we would take a day to fast and pray and see if we hear anything from God. As we wanted time alone and quiet, we decided that we would fill the gas tank and drive about Central Alberta for eight hours.

We got up the next morning, told my sister that we would be back after dinner and left. Paul just started driving. We drove. We stopped where we wanted to. We walked. We prayed together. We prayed alone. We read the Bible together. We read the Bible alone. However, we did not talk at all about what we felt God might be saying to us. We had decided beforehand that we would not talk about anything until we broke our fast after eight hours and while we were eating a late dinner. It was a great day. Very peaceful. It was great to spend the time alone together just enjoying the day and spending time with God all day long.

As 8:00 came about, we stopped in a town called Three Hills for dinner. We entered the restaurant, got a table, accepted menus, then placed our orders. We had hardly spoken. Our fast and prayer time was over. It was time to talk. Paul started. He asked me if I felt that God had spoken to me and, if so, what? I had felt strongly that God told me something but the human side of me had doubts. However, now was not the time for doubts. Now was the time to share with my husband what I felt and thought.

"Yes, I do think that God spoke. It was just two letters but it was multiple times today. DR. DR as in the Dominican Republic." I then went on to explain that I had thoughts since God laid the DR on my mind about that email that we had dismissed from YWAM Dominican Republic. I felt that we were to respond to that email and see if the opportunity to go to the Dominican Republic with YWAM was still an option.

Paul was silent for a bit. I sipped my coke while I waited for him to speak. Finally, Paul took a sip of his coffee and then started to speak. Although, his words were few. Paul said that what I described was basically exactly the same experiences that he had today. WOW to us, this was huge. We decided to go back to my sister's house and write an email to YWAM Dominican Republic immediately and see what happens. The funny thing is that we actually had to look up the geographical location of the Dominican Republic on a map. We did not know exactly where in the world the country was located.

That evening, I wrote an email to YWAM Dominican Republic, explaining about our journey the past few months (as we felt it was important to be honest about this with them) and then asking if they were still interested in us, as a couple, to come to the DR and join their staff?

The next morning, we checked our email and there was a reply from YWAM Dominican Republic. In short, it said yes! Yes, they were still interested in us. Yes, they would like us to come to the Dominican Republic to serve our Lord under YWAM Dominican Republic. We both sat there, reading this email, stunned! It was time to move on and we were going in a different direction than the one that we had been so convinced was the right path.

We later came to describe this period as us being stubborn until God hit us over our heads with a baseball bat and we finally listened to HIM!

Paul called the head Elder of our church in Victoria and explained the last 24 hours to him. We needed the approval of our church and we wanted the opinion of our Elders. Paul and Mr. Rice had a good, long talk. When Paul hung up, we both knew that our journey to foreign missions was about to take off. Mr. Rice spoke to the rest of the Elders of our church and they all approved this decision. Our church was 100% behind us in sending us off to the foreign mission field in the Dominican Republic.

We then spoke with my sister to tell her all about this. We waited until after dinner and after her kids had gone to bed. My sister was thrilled for us. In hindsight, I sometimes wonder if she was more thrilled for us finally knowing what we were going to do or to finally have us out of her house. She never said anything at all and I am so thankful for how she and her husband let us stay with them for four months. I am not sure that I could have done that and I thank God for giving them the grace they needed to put up with us.

Now the real work began. We still could not go anywhere without full monthly support and we were currently at 25%. We needed money for airfare, to purchase plane tickets, sell our car, find someplace to store some of our stuff, figure out what we needed as far as legally entering and staying in the Dominican Republic and getting our affairs in order to be leaving North America.

We made a list of all that we had to complete before we could board a plane. Then, we tackled that list. First on the list was spending time in prayer and talking with God about what His plan is so that we could follow His plan. It would only be with prayer that everything would come together the way God had planned. We had just learned the hard way that when we try to follow our plan, it does not work. You are just hitting your head against the wall.

We then contacted everyone that we knew to share our new plans to move to the Dominican Republic and ministry under YWAM. We were amazed at people's responses. We received many positive emails, letters and phone calls. Some churches invited us to share with their congregations where we were headed. In a matter of weeks, we went from 25% monthly support to 80%. It is amazing what God can do once we step out of His way.

We contacted the Dominican Embassy in Ontario, Canada and learned what we needed to legally enter the country and then to stay in the country long term. We would enter the country on a tourist visa which is purchased at the airport upon arrival in the DR. Then, after being there for a bit, we would have to apply for a residency which take a couple years to obtain.

Next, we had to sell our car. We placed ads and a potential buyer contacted us right away. This buyer even agreed to make the purchase and take possession on the same day that we were planning to catch a plane to the DR. This was such a blessing as then we had use of our car until the moment that we were ready to leave the country.

Now we had to get plane tickets. We headed to a travel agent to find out what options were available to fly from Alberta to the Dominican Republic. It was suggested by YWAM to fly into the capital city, Santo Domingo, as that is where the YWAM office is located. We discovered that the difference in price between flying into Santo Domingo or Puerto Plata was substantial. We opted to fly into Puerto Plata because it was about $200 cheaper per ticket. In 1995, that was a lot of money. We would be flying from Edmonton to Toronto to Puerto Plata.

It was a whirlwind as the days flew by. A new friend offered to store some of our stuff at their farm. The car sold. We went through our stuff and narrowed things down to two suitcases each. Got our paperwork and banking stuff all in order. Plane tickets were purchased. Financial support was starting to come in. With the sale of the car, that gave us some cash on hand to be able to get started in life in the DR.

Five weeks after we had taken a day to drive around Central Alberta for a day of prayer and fasting, we were at the Edmonton Airport, saying our byes to my sister and her family, and boarding a plane to the Dominican Republic. Five weeks! Once we got out of God's way, started to follow God's plans and not ours, things happened quickly and we were off to start our time as foreign missionaries to the Dominican Republic.

"*Exalt the Lord our God and worship at his holy mountain, for the Lord our God is holy.*"

Psalm 99:9

27 June 1997

Arrival in the Dominican Republic

As we stepped off the plane in this new land that God has called us to, the air hit us like a brick wall. It is almost 10 pm at night, local time and the air is so thick with humidity that you would think that you could cut it with a knife. Neither one of us had ever felt tropical humidity before and nothing can prepare you for that. We looked around at the clear night, stars and moon reflecting off the Atlantic Ocean as we follow the line of departing passengers across the tarmac to the airport building. Within the first couple minutes, we already know that this is nothing like home. Where has God sent us?

We enter the airport terminal from the tarmac and follow the crowd towards the immigration officers. We fill out the immigration paperwork, get our passports stamps and proceed to pick up our luggage. God told us that we were to follow Him, He will take care of us; to pack up everything and move to this island country to serve Him. We brought the airline limit for our luggage which includes four bags of 70 pounds each and two carry on pieces. We are heavily loaded. As we wait for our bags to come down the carousal, we pray that all our bags are there. Our destination is the other side of the island so we do not want to have to return to this airport to find lost luggage. Praise God, all our luggage arrived with us. We load up the carts and proceed through Customs. The

Custom officers hardly give us a glance as we proceed out the door and to find ourselves outside and back into that air cutting humidity.

There is a crowd of people, some with signs to pick up people that they do not know which includes us. We have been told by the director of the ministry that a pastor will be there to pick us up. We had no idea what the pastor would look like, who to look for or even his name. As we looked about, I am sure that the local people were watching at as and thinking about how lost we appeared. A man with a piece of paper with our names scribbled on it stepped towards us, pointing to the sign. We said "Yes, that is us. Are you here to pick us up?" The kind looking man just smiled at us and spoke in Spanish. Oh Oh - we do not speak or understand any Spanish and it appears that this man picking us up did not speak or understand English. What are we going to do now? "Well Lord, we are in Your hands", I think to myself. I look at my husband and he seems to have the same look on his face as I do.

This nice man with a paper with our names on it holds up his hand, gesturing for us to stay put. He goes forward to talk with a taxi driver. It seems like a small argument is going on as the taxi driver and the man picking us up go back and forth. The man walks away from the driver and it is clear that no deal has been made. The man returns to us, smiles and motions for us to stay put. We stand there, in the dark, in the humidity, waiting but we have no idea what we are waiting for. Ten minutes pass and more people leave the airport. Twenty minutes pass and there are now even less people at the airport. Thirty minutes pass and it seems that we are about the only people left at the airport. We are getting nervous. It is near 11:00 pm and we are almost all alone in a strange country, with a stranger, not speaking the language and not a clue as to what to do. It is 1997 and hardly anyone owns a cell phone. The man turns, smiles at us then goes to talk to another driver. The man comes back, starts to push our luggage towards a beat up car (one that we think is ready for the junk yard) and our luggage is being loaded into the car. Then the man motions us for money. We have no idea what to do or pay. The man reaches into the wallet, pulls out an amount of money and hands half to the driver. He then motions for us to get into the car with the rest of our luggage piled on our laps.

We start to drive away from the airport, it is near 11:30pm and we have no idea where we are going and if we are in danger. It is a very good thing that God is in control because we certainly know that we are not.

After about twenty minutes, we see the lights of a city appear and I breathe a bit better. Things can not be too bad if we are going into the city. We must be going to the house of the pastor, the man who has picked us up at the airport. As I look out the window, wondering what I am looking at, I notice that we turn away from the city lights. Oh-Oh - where are we going and will we be safe. "God, you got us this far, I am sure that you will keep us safe, right?"

We continue to drive for about another thirty minutes. The driver turns down one road, then another. The roads can hardly be called roads; there are so many potholes and some parts of the road are hardly wide enough for one vehicle. I guess that it is a good thing that we have not seen another car for more than ten minutes. However, at this thought, I get a little fear in the pit of my stomach. The driver turns down another road and all of sudden, out of nowhere, we seem to be in some kind of a neighbourhood. It is obvious that it is a poor area but at least there is civilization, houses, people. We stop outside a building that is lit up and there is a lot of music. It is late at night so it must be some kind of a celebration or party. The pastor/the man who picked us up at the airport jumps out of the car, without a look back at us, runs inside the building. Oh-Oh - what is going to happen to us now, I wonder? After about five minutes, five very long, long minutes, the man returns, jumps back into the car and says something to the driver and we are off again. We go left, right, left.... back and forth until I think that we are driving in circles then stop in front of a row of houses. The man jumps out, the driver gets out, they pop the trunk, start taking out our bags and putting them in front of a house that has a small porch. We look at each other wondering what is going on. Then our door opens and the man gestures for us to get out. We do. What else would we do?

It is clear that no one is home at this house. It is dark, locked up and we are on the porch with this man and our bags as the car drives away once the man gave the driver the other half of our money. We stand on this porch, looking at this man, wondering what is going on. He just continues to smile at us and tries to gesture that all is okay. It must be after midnight by now. The minutes tick by and we have no idea what is going on. After what seemed like hours but was probably only about twenty minutes, a scooter pulls up with a couple on it. They park the scooter and the man approaches us. He opens his mouth to speak and the sweetest sound came out...... English. "Welcome to my home and my country" this man says to us. We look at each other, breathe a sigh of relief and shake this man's hand and then his wife's hand. The English speaking man says something to the other man in Spanish and then the man who had brought us here from the airport shakes our hands and says "Adios" and he is gone.

It turns out that the man who went to the airport to get us was a friend and not the pastor. The English speaking man is the pastor and we are staying in his home tonight. In the morning, he will get us on the bus to travel the six hours south to the Capital city - our final destination. The pastor welcomes us to his home, shows us to his bedroom, where the bathroom is and says good night. With that, we are alone in this concrete house that, by what we are use to, is very poor and just a shack. We have no water, nothing to drink or eat and know that we are on our own until morning. We thank God that we are safe.

In the morning, the pastor and his wife are waiting for us. They ask if we are hungry or thirsty and offer us a breakfast of warm coke cola and dry bread. We are thankful for both. The pastor apologizes for not coming to the airport himself but he had church service. Where we had stopped on the way was his church and they have church services five nights a week. Once we finish eating, he explains that he will take us to the bus stop. And another adventure begins..............

March 1998 – Excerpt from Our Newsletters

As vehicles are so expensive here, there are more motorcycles, scooters, etc. on the road than vehicles. However, no one really knows how to drive well or obey road rules. Driving here is very dangerous. It is common to see 4 or 5 people on a motorbike. Babies hanging off mother's hips and kids standing in front of the Dad who is driving the bike. No one wears a helmet and people drive with their bottle of beer or rum open in their hands. We are so very thankful that God has protected us and kept us safe every time that we have been in a vehicle.

September 1998

Excerpt from Our Newsletters

God Multiplies His Children

In the mountains of the northeastern part of the Dominican Republic is a small village called *Los Hidaljas*. There is one small church and on this Friday evening, we are here with an evangelistic group of 35 youths from the US & Canada. The team has 2 minute skits, a testimony, a 20 minute drama, another testimony and then the local pastor gives a short message and an altar call. The crowd that has gathered is about 200 people. The youth are all nervous as they wait their turn to either perform in a skit, drama or give their testimony. We can feel God's presence with each skit and testimony. The crowd loves the skits and drama. There are a few weepy eyes during the testimony then their pastor speaks followed by asking if anyone wants to give their lives to Jesus Christ, right now, tonight!

A few kids raise their hands, then a few adults, a mother, a sister, then *the* old man comes forward. (In Dominican culture, the oldest man in the village sets the stage for what is right and wrong, what you can do and can not do.) When the old man came forward to accept Jesus into his heart as Lord and Saviour, it was an incredible witness to the rest of the village.

After the old man came forward, then more came forward and in this small village, that had one Christian at 5:00 pm that Friday evening, by 8:00 pm, now has 35 Christians.

"Be exalted, O Lord, in your strength, we will sing and praise your might."

Psalm 21:13

22 September 1998

Hurricane Georges

Hurricane Georges became a hurricane on 15 September 1998 as it moved west across the Atlantic Ocean. It was a category 4 hurricane before it hit any land. By the time Hurricane Georges hit the island of Hispaniola and the Dominican Republic on 22 September, it had lost some strength. It hit Puerto Rico, leaving death and destruction in its path. It did lose some strength over Puerto Rico and dropped to a category 3 hurricane by the time it made landfall in the Dominican Republic.

At this time, the Dominican Republic did not have a strong method of informing the public of hurricanes. We had the local radio turned on and did not hear warning for our area until the hurricane was already hitting our area. It was the same poor level of public communication all across the country.

On September 2, 1998, we had moved from the YWAM base to our own house. For over a year, we had been living in community, at the YWAM base. God had provided everything that we needed in order to rent a house in the nearest town of Jarabacoa. We took possession and moved into a very modest, small house that was made of brick with a tin roof. There was nothing fancy about it but it met all our basic needs. When we moved in, we had very little. YWAM lent us a couple sort of couches that had actually been bench seating on a ship. We borrowed a plastic folding table from YWAM and two plastic chairs until we could purchase a table and chair of our own. Our landlord gave us a rocking chair, a small area rug and few things for the kitchen. We were happy and looking forward to creating a home for ourselves on the mission field.

Nineteen days after we moved to the house, there starts to be talk around town that a hurricane is on its way and the Dominican Republic is right in its path. We did not have television nor internet. (Internet was not available at private homes yet in the Dominican Republic.) We did have a small, short wave radio that we were able to listen to the local radio station on. When we returned to the house on 21 September, we decided to prepare a bit in case the storm did hit. Paul went to town to buy a couple 5 gallon bottles of water. We moved what small number of personal items into the closets. The two closets in the house were built of brick and concrete with concrete roofs on the closets. These were the only spots in the house that provided any protection for our personal items. Then, we went to bed.

As the night went on, the weather did worsen but it was not at storm level. In the morning, we woke early and looked outside. The sky was dark and looked "mean". The wind was picking up and there was starting to be a small amount of rain. Missionary friends lived two blocks from us and called to see how we were doing. Our missionary friends were renting a fully concrete house so they had no worries of losing their roof. Their concern was potential flooding on the first floor. Our concern was the roof as we had a tin roof that could easily be ripped off. Our friends told us that if we want to wait out the storm at their house, that we were welcome to. We told them that if the storm got bad and it looked like we may lose our roof, we would come up to their house.

About two hours later, the wind and rain really picked up. We finally heard warnings on the radio for our area. The warnings said that the eye of the storm would be going over us and that everyone should seek higher ground and concrete buildings to take refuge in. We went through our house to make sure that anything that could get damaged was in a closet and that the closets were locked with a padlock. Paul checked that all the windows were closed as best as possible. We had metal lever windows. A strong wind and rain could bring water inside the house. The doors were closed. We had nothing lose outside. Now, we just waited for the storm to get worse and prayed. In about an hour, we knew that we were experiencing our first hurricane. We did not know what category it was but we had heard a couple days earlier that it was up to a category 4 storm. The rain pelted against the metal lever windows. The rain was so strong on the tin roof that we could not hear each other talk when we only inches away from each other. Neither one of us had ever seen wind and rain like this before. It seemed like the rain and wind were coming at us from every direction. We had raining coming in through the slats on the windows on all four sides of the house, at the same time!

Then, we heard a weird sound coming from the living room. It was coming from the roof at the southwest corner of the house. We looked up and saw outside. The roof was starting to peel back. The wind had torn the nails loose at the corner of the roof (about a 5' x 10' area) and the tin was getting lifted up by the winds then slapping back down. Either the wind would win and tear the whole roof or it would stay as it is with the corner of the roof flapping in the wind and the rain continuing to pour into the living room. Either way, we decided that we did not want to stick around and see what would happen. We agreed to head to our mission friends' house.

We had already packed a backpack with our necessitates in it. Bibles, books, clothing for a few days, toiletries, passports, visas and other important documents. We put on our shoes, rain coats, grabbed the backpack, locked the front door and headed out to walk to our friends' house. Normally, it would take us about five minutes to walk from our house to their house. Today, it would take us much longer.

As we stepped out into the storm, we had no idea how strong the weather was going to be. Coming from Western Canada, we had only heard about hurricanes as a footnote in the news of something that happened in Florida. In hindsight, we really should have stayed put at our house, but, we did not. We started to walk up the dirt road from our house to the next street. The road was now a very fast flowing creek with about six to eight inches of water covering the entire dirt road. We made it to the end of this road where we had to turn left to walk about 200 metres to the next road. On this road is only one house and some pasture fields. As we are walking along, we are trying to stay close but at one point, we end up being about five feet part. Right at this moment, we hear a loud crack, feel something flying down on us. We feel the ground shake with a huge, loud, THUD. I instantly turn around to see that a very large tree has fallen right behind me. It has missed me by less than a couple inches, literally. I call out for Paul as I cannot see him. This huge tree with all its branches are too tall and I cannot see over it. I call and call. Finally, over the wind and the rain, I hear Paul. He is on the other side of the fallen tree. The tree also missed Paul by just a couple inches. It fell right between us at the only moment in the entire walk that we were not walking right close together. WOW God is taking very good care of us!

This has totally freaked us out and we just want to get to safety. We turn up the next road and are now within sight of our friends' home. We run as best as we can while jumping over and going around tress, branches and wading through inches and inches of rain water. Finally, we arrive! We knock on the door and our friends let us in. We are soaked, tired and freaked out. It took us almost 45 minutes to walk less than a quarter mile!

Once dried off and feeling safe, we all hunker down to ride out the storm. Our friends have three teenagers so the seven of us sit around playing cards, board games and chatting until we all decide to go to bed. As we head to bed, the storm is still raging. We find out later that the eye of the storm did go right over our heads. We experienced the front of the hurricane, then the calm of the eye of the storm, then the anger of the back side of the storm. The back side of the storm was fiercer than the front and left even more damage everywhere.

In the morning, we all rise early. No one could sleep well. Around 4 am, the storm had calmed. Come 7 am, the humidity level was rising quickly, the sun was out and everyone was coming out of their homes to survey the damage. As we headed to the side road that the house was on, we could not tell where property stopped and road began. We walked to the end of the street to see the main road. This road is one of the main artery roads of the town. Where was the road? All that we could see was fallen trees, blown branches and debris that piled over ten feet high across the entire road and as far as the eye could see. It was amazing!

Men were out everywhere with their machetes. No one was waiting around for the government to clear roads. Everyone knew that we all had to pitch in if any of us wanted to get anywhere. Within two hours, and many hands working hard, the main road was cleared of debris so that there was now one side open. Motorbikes were already screaming by. We were shocked at how fast our neighbours were getting the mess of the storm cleaned up and that no one was waiting on the government to do it. Obviously, the local people had been through storms like this before and are used to taking care of themselves. They taught us a lot on this day about truly helping and loving your neighbour.

We worked with our friends and neighbours to clear away debris from the roads around their home. After lunch, we all headed down to our house to see if we still had a roof. With machetes in hands, we made the trek. It was easier today than it was in the middle of the hurricane. The sun was out, it was hot, and paths had already been cleared on these little dirt roads. A motorbike could get by. Someone walking could get past. However, a vehicle could not use the roads yet.

As we walked, we chopped away some debris. We got to the top of the little hill that preceded our house and started down the hill. We could see our property but not the actual house yet. One of our neighbours was out clearing debris and asked if we had been to our house yet. We said that we had not and our neighbour said not to worry, he would help us. He left what he was doing to come with us. As the house came into view, the first thing that we noticed was that the roof was still on the house and no trees had landed on the house. There were downed trees and debris everywhere but not on the house. Our neighbour helped us as we cut and cleared away debris so that we could open the gate to the property and get to the house. Just like our neighbours, there was plenty of branches and debris but the house looked good. As we unlocked the house and entered, we discovered that the living room had flooded due to the corner of the roof being uplifted in the storm. However, besides the small amount of flooding and corner of the roof needing repair, the house was fine! Praise God!

Paul, our friend and our neighbour quickly tackled the job of nailing down the roof while us ladies did some mopping and cleaning inside the house. In less than two hours, our house was livable! At this point, we left our house to help some of our neighbours.

The men discovered that the water to the street had been damaged and would need repair. We all learned the road at the bottom of the mountain washed out so our area was on its own for a while. Until the government repaired the road, no vehicle could pass and bring up supplies. There was no electricity. There was no water. There were no supply trucks on its way.

The ice factory opened twice a day for 90 minutes at a time. Each family was allowed to buy two bags of ice twice a day. We used this ice to keep our food from rotting and to drink when the ice melted.

We had no running water or electricity to our house. Once the roads were cleared enough for a car, we headed out to buy gas for the car and generator as well as to find some water. Word was out about the washed out road which meant that the only gas available was what the three gas stations in town had on hand. The line ups at the gas stations were hours long! But, just like everyone else, we needed gas in the car and to fill up as many jerry cans that we could with gas in order to run a generator. So, like everyone else, we waited hours and hours in the line at the gas station.

After getting gas, we went to the river to fill jugs with water. This water was not drinkable but, with some bleach, we could use it to wash dishes, clean, flush toilets and bathe in. We were very thankful for a car so that we could haul water without having to carry it for miles. We were borrowing a car from missionary friends who were on a six-month furlough.

As the days went on, everyone got into a routine. Twice a day, someone from the households would stand in line at the ice factory to buy their allotted two bags of ice and one 5 gallon bottle of water. Water would be hauled from the river to fill jugs, buckets and barrels around the house. Cleaning, washing, showering was done with as minimal water possible. Laundry was done every day because every article of clothing had to be washed by hand. You did not want to pile up a few days of laundry or it would take you all day to wash clothes. Jeans, towels and sheets became the dreaded items to wash as they were large, heavy and so hard to rinse out. But - we were thankful to have some water to be able to wash with.

When it rained, all the buckets were put outside to catch the rain running off the tin roofs. Anything that could hold any amount of water were put outside. Water really had become everyone's gold. In a good down pour, we would put on our bathing suits, grab the soap and shampoo and head outside. Under the run off from the roof, we would have the best shower that we had had since the last rain. No conserving water and trying to bathe in less than a gallon of water! As we would look around, we would spot our neighbours outside, showering in the run off from their roofs. It was all quite funny to look at, when you could forget that the real reason for all of us showering outside like this was because we were months without running water.

We still had no electricity so as the sun set, out came the lanterns and candles. The rest of the evening would take place by candle and lantern light. Many times, we felt that we living in early settler days. One thing that we quickly learned is that water is a necessity; electricity is a luxury. We *needed* water. We did not need electricity. It really was not as hard to live without electricity as one would think. Your schedule does change as you ensure that you get done during daylight hours is what you could not do by candlelight and you put off until the evening what you did not need a lot of light for.

After three months of living without electricity, one day the lights came on!!! You could hear people screaming in joy all over the place. The washed out road at the bottom of the mountain was fixed about a month after the hurricane. Once this happened, work and supply trucks could make it up the mountain. We were very thankful to have electricity return. Although electricity is not a necessity; it does make many things a lot easier to accomplish and life just a little easier.

Now that we had electricity, the prayer for water to reach our house became even stronger. So many water lines had been damaged and destroyed in the hurricane. About four months after the hurricane, we started to hear about certain parts of the town proper having their water return. We were very hopeful. The government was working on returning water sector by sector. Our house was just outside of the town proper but still within one of these sectors. As we were still somewhat new to the country (just under two years), we were still learning language and culture.

After about ten months, we noticed that our neighbours were no longer hauling water and had water to their homes. However, we still did not have any running water coming to our property. For ten months now, we had been living with no running water and hauling every ounce of water that we consumed. Paul decided to go by our landlady to speak to her about the water. When Paul returned home, he was not too happy. He explained that the government had not fixed the water pipes to our street yet and that it would be six to twelve months before water was restored. However, our neighbours have water because they all got together, pitching in equal shares of money and work and dug a well. Once the well was dug, every neighbour who contributed labour and money were able to tap into the well and now had running water in their homes. Our landlady explained that she did not see the point in joining the neighbours in this project and she was not able to contribute any labour.

This was not good news to us. Paul explained to the landlady that if she had approached us, Paul would have gladly volunteered his time and labour and we could have even helped with some of the financial costs. It was well worth it to us in order to have running water to our house. Plus, now that the neighbours had solved their own water problem, the government dropped our road down on the list to get fixed. After one year, we still had no running water to our house and were still hauling every ounce of water that we needed and showering in the rain.

It was coming time for us to head back to Canada for our first furlough. We had gone to the Dominican Republic in June 1997. It was now Fall 1999 and time to touch base with our supporters and to see family. We prayed about and decided to give notice to our landlady. Friends said that we could store our minimal possessions at their house while we were in Canada. Another friend was going to be on furlough for three more weeks when we returned from Canada so we agreed to house sit for them. This was a huge blessing because it gave us a place to stay when we returned from Canada and three weeks to find a house to rent. So - we gave notice, moved our stuff to our friends' house and headed to Canada for seven weeks. At the time that we moved out of the house, it had been over a year since Hurricane George hit and we still had no running water to the property and house.

29 September 1998

San Juan de la Maguana, one week after Hurricane George hit.

At this time, we were missionaries with Youth With A Mission (YWAM). It is September 1998, one week after Hurricane Georges devastated the Dominican Republic Haiti, leaving thousands dead and hundreds of thousands homeless. YWAM had many resources and made the decision to head the part of the country worst hit by Hurricane George. It was decided a day trip would be made as housing was scarce in the most damaged areas. So many people were homeless. There certainly was no place for a mission group to be housed. YWAM was going to deliver food, water, clothing and medical supplies. I was licensed to drive a small bus and with my medical background, I was one of the people asked to go on this trip. Paul did not go on this trip.

We had all heard the reports of how bad things were in the San Juan de la Maguana area. San Juan is located between two large rivers. When Hurricane George hit, the water level of these two rivers rose so high that they basically rose above the town and came crashing down on top of the town and the people. There were no final numbers of how many people died the night of the hurricane but it was being estimated at around 5000 people. Pretty much, all survivors were displaced from their homes; many of whom lost their homes and all their possession in the hurricane.

We left Santo Domingo at about 5 am to make the three hour drive out to San Juan. We were in two vehicles. The drive out to San Juan was basically smooth. Most of the roads were still intact and those that had received damage from the hurricane had either been repaired or temporarily repaired that it did not create long delays. At least it was like this until about 10 km outside of the town proper. Then, the road just disappeared. It was completely gone. The route that was now "road" was all dried up mud that had been displaced and left from the hurricane. There were mounds were there never was. We were traveling at about 10 km per hour as we basically drove a route that would make any outback, 4x4, bush whacking route look like a regular road. It took us over about 90 minutes to drive about 10 kilometers.

When we finally arrived in San Juan, we all became speechless. Up until now, there was plenty of conversation about what we were witnessing, the lack of road, what we were driving upon, etc. Now there were no words. The devastation and death was beyond words. The first thing that we noticed was the smell. There was a very distinct smell. It was hard for some people to identify but to me, I knew immediately what it was. I had smelt this before. It was the smell of death. Dead rats, dead cats, dead dogs, dead horses, dead people. There really are no words to describe the aroma of death but it is an aroma that one never forgets. Ever!

As I drove the bus into the city of San Juan, people were wandering everywhere and the roads were hard to distinguish. There were some areas of organized chaos where the government, organizations and other ministries were already on the ground helping the local survivors. Then, there were so many people who just seemed to be wondering around aimlessly, not knowing what to do or where to go. I would soon learn that these people were aimless. They had lost all that they owned, lost loved ones and really did not know where to go or what to do. I was struggling to understanding how it would feel to find yourself in this position. Yesterday, life was normal and today, you had nothing at all. God quickly reminded me that no matter what we lose of physical possessions, and loved ones that we lose, God will always remain right there beside us. He is walking beside us in good times, holding our hands in tough times, carrying and cradling us in the really hard moments of life. God is with us!

We reached our destination in the town and opened our doors. The smell instantly hit us all. The smell is so hard to explain yet, it is worse than dead skunk. It is unique. It burns your nostrils and curdles your stomach. It is the smell of death. Rotting flesh of every kind was everywhere and the smell was thick in the air. Animals, people, food..... death was everywhere. Since this day, when I have smelt a dead rat or something like this, I am instantly transported back to this time to San Juan. I had never smelt death to this extent before.

We started to unload the food, water and supplies that we had brought to the local church that we going to be working with. What we thought was a lot of food, water and supplies when we left Santo Domingo, now seems so little and insufficientt. The needs are so great that I even wondered how our amount of food and supplies could even help. But, it did help as it did give clothes to some, drinking water and food for a few days to numerous people. It helped people survive for a few more days until more supplies could reach this devastated town.

Part of our goal was to provide comfort and prayer for survivors. After unloading all our supplies to the local church, some stayed to help organize and distribute and some of us headed out to walk about and see where else we could help. We walked down what once was a road, and now it was just mud piled 12 – 24 inches above the pavement. All that mud had come from the rivers. We were walking on ground/mud that was about two feet higher than the road. As we walked, I saw half of a horse sticking up out of the mud. The mud came crashing down on top of many animals who were buried alive. This horse's front half was buried with his bottom half sticking up out of the mud. We also saw dogs like this. The local people told us stories of friends, neighbours, loved ones, who had also been buried under mud that came crashing down like huge waves.

I was invited into the remains of one house by the father. His family, thankfully, had survived but the house was destroyed. The roof was blown off. Mud had crashed down on the house after the roof blew off. The mud that was left buried half the house while every wall was covered in mud. There were clothes still hanging on hangers on hooks on the walls, bathed and dried in mud. It was beyond surreal. The father was praising God because his family survived. All of his neighbours' houses looked the same or worse than his but, as this man shared, he was blessed because many of this neighbours did not survive.

The hurricane does not know age, or economic status. People of all ages, from infants to the elderly were killed. No one really knows how many people died the day Hurricane George hit the Dominican Republic. It is estimated that over 5000 died just in San Juan de la Maguana and about 10,000 across the entire country. Over 750,000 people lost their homes that day and it took years before a new "normal" to life was established for many of the survivors.

What we witnessed and lived through during Hurricane George is no different than what people all over the world live through when a hurricane, typhoon, tsunami or earthquake hits their home. Natural disasters are very devastating and destroy lives. Our prayer is that even though people have to suffer through natural disasters, that when they do endure such hardship, people's faith grows.

"Whatever we do, it is because Christ's love controls us."

2 Corinthians 5:14

Natural Disasters

In our near two decades living in the Dominican Republic, we have experienced every natural disaster except for a snow storm.

We have been awoken by numerous earthquakes. One night, we were awakened at 1:19 am, looked outside and saw the water pipe that came up outside of our bedroom window swaying at 40 degrees, back and forth. Three days later when we went to the city of Santiago, once stores had re-opened, I walked into the grocery store and was assaulted by the strong smell of stale alcohol. It smelled like a bar after a week of solid partying. It was all due to all the alcohol that had fallen off shelves and broken in the earthquake. Praise God that the earthquake was in the middle of the night, with the stores, empty and not full of people that could have been injured/hit by these falling bottles.

One afternoon, all of a sudden, the sky turned grey and then the sound of the wind started. Almost instantly, we had rain blowing in every window of the house, on all four sides. We did not realize it right away but we were right in the middle of a tornado. Thanks be to God, the tornado did not last long and, besides some broken trees, there was no damage.

We have experienced earthquakes from 3.3 to 7.0. Every year we have various tropical storms; some years those storms grow into hurricanes. Tornados are more common than people imagine here. We have floods and damage from water and mud.

Through all of these natural disasters, God has protected us from harm and damage to our properties. God is so good and always takes such good care of us.

February 1999

Six Houses in Seven days and 500 Patients

For two weeks in February 1999, we hosted a short term mission team from Minnesota with seven of those days being spent in the mountains of Neyba, Dominican Republic. This team brought two main skills. Some of the team had a medical back ground and some of the team had a construction background. This team was the perfect fit for Paul and as that is exactly what our skills are. We rented the World Vision camp facility which had a kitchen, dining area, multi purpose building and cabins. This village in the mountains is a very poor village. It is isolated and the people have very little. Most houses are dirt floors with palm bark for exterior walls.

Paul lead the construction team and set out with a goal of building six houses in seven days. The houses would be built on a concrete slab, with plywood walls and tin roofs. The team came equipped with all the tools that they would need and we had generators for the power tools. Even though these houses were very simple, they were a lot better than the lean-to shacks that these families were currently living in.

I led a two-day medical clinic while the construction guys were building houses. We spent on day preparing before we opened the doors of the multi purpose building to have the medical clinic. On the first day, I had a general physician, an optometrist, a nurse working with me. On the second day, I had a dentist, an optometrist, a pediatrician and two general physicians. In those two days, we saw a huge variety medical problems and many people in need. We saw over 500 general patients, 154 eye patients and 42 dental patients. We gave out a lot of free medication and health education. All the while, we were sharing the Word of God with the patients and their families.

September 2000

Excerpt from Our Newsletters

Baby's First Breath

In June/July, we hosted another medical team and went to the Barahona area. It was a small team so we just did the surgical and dental work. The hospital that we were working in is a small, rural hospital. When we arrived one morning, the local doctor was just finishing a caesarean section. As we arrived, the nurse was bringing the new baby out of the OR and the baby in respiratory distress. There were no other doctors on staff at this hour. Our doctor, Dr. Julio Gomez, and I quickly took the baby and started to work on this newborn. (I was not even changed into my scrubs yet.) After about 20 minutes and help from our anaesthesiologist, Dr. Jose Abreu, we were able to get this little baby breathing and starting to pink up. It was such a blessing to be able to work along side the local staff and get this little one breathing without difficulties.

January 2001

Excerpt from Our Newsletters

Trip Through San Fran

We had only been in the country about three years by this time and serving with MMI for about a year. It is 4 am and the alarm clock went off. We had thirty minutes to get up, get ready, grab a quick bite to eat and get out the door. We are expected in Nagua before 8 am and it is at least a three hour drive. We will be going through San Francisco de Marcoris rather than Puerto Plata along the coast, as it is quicker route. We know the coastal route better, but that would add almost two hours to the drive time. Paul asks me to drive as he is sleepy, needing coffee and, as I am not a coffee drinker, I feel wide awake already. It will be about an hour to reach San Fran and then about two hours from there to Nagua.

In Nagua, we will be meeting up with the medical team from MMI in order to work with them, helping in the leadership and work of this mission for the next two weeks. The team flew in on Saturday but we had commitments at our local church so our boss, Teo, said it would be fine to meet them in Nagua before the team headed out on Monday morning. We hoped to make good enough time to arrive at breakfast time.

From our house in Jarabacoa down to San Fran, it was a smooth trip, uneventful, and little traffic at this hour. It was dark when we left the house and we watch the sun rise as we drive east toward San Fran. San Fran is an older town that, when it grew, it seems that road was put in just wherever. There seems to be no logic to the roads as you try to make your way from one side of town to the other. We have only been to San Fran a couple times so we do not know the route through the town well. I knew that we had to come to a T-intersection, turn left and then take a right. I made the left and then took a right hand turn. Immediately, I saw that I had turned onto a dead end street and made a wrong turn. I stopped our vehicle, put it in reverse and then looked over my shoulder to start backing up. At that moment - I saw guns in the back window. I looked forward and saw more guns. All around us, there were guns pointed at us. As we sat there, I quickly counted. 21 guns were aimed at us by 21 men in uniforms.

When God is protecting you, sometimes, it seems that we just act and are not thinking at all. This is what I felt. As I looked back, I cannot remember actually thinking anything at all. I lowered my window, looked into the barrel of a gun and a not too friendly looking police officer and said "Donde esta la calle a Nagua?" (Where is the road to Nagua?). I have no idea what the police officers were thinking but the one right by my window waved the other officers to lower their guns and then he pointed the direction to me. He then called out to two officers and said "follow them - they will show you the way. Do not stop anywhere and do nothing except follow them. They will take you to the highway to Nagua." I said thank you, put up my window, backed up and followed the officers until we were just outside of San Fran and we saw a sign that said the way to Nagua.

Paul and I hardly spoke during all this. As we started to follow the officers, the effect of having all those guns pointed us started to hit home. Fear started to kick in but we just kept praying and thanking God for protecting us.

Two hours later, we arrive at the camp in Nagua; arriving as the team is eating breakfast. Our boss, Teo, comes over to us to greet us and gives us a hug. He asked how the drive went and Paul and I just look at each other. By this time, a couple other of the Dominican staff have come over to say hi and are listening. Teo sees the looks on our faces and asks what happened. We told him what had happened in San Fran. All our Dominican friends praise God for our safety. One staff said that he had heard on the radio that morning that there had been two prisoners who had escaped from the federal prison in San Fran and huge manhunt was on for them. A vehicle had been waiting for the prisoners - it was the exact same year, make, model and colour as our vehicle! Teo grabs both of us in a two arm hug and says a prayer of thanks. Then he tells us that it is a miracle that we are alive! In the DR, in cases such as a manhunt, the police always shoot first, ask questions later. They never hesitate, wait for a car window to be put down or anything. They just shoot!

Once again, God was with us and protected us the entire time. Even in our naive knowledge of the culture and the fact that a massive manhunt was on, God protected us.

"Call to Me, and I will answer you, and show you great and mighty things, which you do not know."

Jeremiah 33:3

2001

Best Christmas Presents Ever, Part I

Paul and I married in 1991. We were young; only 22 and 23 years old. Both of us were still working towards our university degrees and on our careers while trying to figure out with God what He wanted us to be when we grew up. After school, missionary training, serving God in various countries and then settling in the Dominican Republic, we were finally able to think about starting a family. It was late 1997 when we made this decision. After a few years, various doctor visits, etc, we learned that we have very low chances of ever getting pregnant. The past few years were an example of that truth.

It is always fascinating to me how I can look back at what God has done in my life and have those "ah-ah" moments where I finally see what God was doing all along. For Paul and I, deciding to adopt and stop trying to get pregnant was a very easy decision because God had already prepared us..... only we did not know this yet. When we had been married for about one year, while we were still so young, in school and the thought of a baby frightened us to no end, we had a discussion about "what would we do if we ever discovered that we could not get pregnant?". We talked for a quite awhile, sharing with each other our thoughts, feelings and opinions on everything from vitamins to fertility drugs to in vitro-fertilization to adoption. When we talked about adoption, we even talked about domestic and international adoption, adopting a different race than ourselves, genders, and ages. After this discussion, we never really thought much about it and life went on.

Fast forward from 1992 to mid-2000 and we find ourselves faced with the fact that we probably will never get pregnant. While dealing with the doctors, our decisions were easy because we had already decided how far we would go, medically, to try to get pregnant before calling it quits and turning to the path of adoption. Our decision had been to go as far as testing, vitamins and such but would stop at ever doing fertility drugs or more. We now found ourselves at this point in life. Next decision was simple.... adoption. We had already made this decision in 1992. We had no idea in 1992 how huge that discussion would then become a paramount part of our lives forever.

For me, I honestly had no problem giving up ever getting pregnant and moving on to the path of adoption. For me, it seems very natural. Paul struggled more with this than I did, but he too, moved to that path of adoption with ease. We were definitely united on this decision and moved forward.

As I am more the logical thinking and researcher in our marriage, I started to research. Being that we are now living in the Dominican Republic, my research had no limits. I was looking at countries all over the world. I started with Canada because, as Canadians, I thought that adoption would be simpler, and less expensive, if we adopted from within our country. I learned that it was not very expensive to adopt in Canada, just the legal fees, medical costs and such. However, the wait list for adoption was huge. At the time, we were quoted as minimum two years for an older child or special need child and minimum six years for a child under the age of two with no special needs. This was disheartening as we did not wait six plus years. We were already 32 years old and has been married for nine years. We did not want to wait until we were late 30s before having our first child. We did not feel God was telling us to adopt a special needs child as we could not provide any type of specialized care or help in the mountains of a third world country.

The international search then grew. I lo,oked at Ethiopia, Russia, China, Romania, Nigeria, Haiti, Dominican Republic, United States, and more. After praying and searching and praying more, we had no idea where to begin. We had ruled out some countries strictly due to costs. Some countries, such as Ethiopia and China, were $30,000 or more just to get things started for an international adoption. We learned that we wanted to adopt from a country that was recognized by The Hague Convention. Countries that are not recognized by The Hague Convention for their adoption process do have their adoption process recognized by Canada. What this means is that we would adopt in the home country of the child and then have to re-adopt the child in Canada. Adoptions done in countries that are recognized by The Hague Convention have the adoptions recognized in Canada. That is a huge saving a not only money, but, time and paperwork.

We were at a loss as to which country to start out with. While we were praying, a new missionary family moved to our area of the Dominican Republic. This family, the Johnsons, had been missionaries for many years in different countries. They had four children and had never adopted. However, they had friends who they met on the mission field who are Canadians and had adopted three children from Haiti. The Johnsons connected us with this family and we were able to talk to them about their adoption. They had a very positive story that they shared with us and it really encouraged us. They gave us the name of the orphanage in Haiti that they adopted from so that we could contact the orphanage to get more information.

Paul and I were both excited as we really felt that God answered our pray with giving us some direction. We reached out to the orphanage in Haiti to obtain some basic information about adoption. This orphanage was being run by an American mother and daughter team and they had a good staff of Haitians who worked at the orphanage. The orphanage is a small orphanage called *Haiti Children Home (HCH)*. We research the orphanage and everything that we discovered was positive. HCH told us that being that we live on the same island, we could adopt directly from them and not have to go through an adoption agency in Canada. This alone was the saving of about $8000 and a lot more paperwork and time.

After lots of prayer, seeking out more counsel and information, Paul and I decided to take the baby steps towards adopting a child from HCH. HCH sent us a list of all the documents that we would have to gather, what would have to be in English and what would need to be in French, and also directed us in where to get some thing completed, such as government approved medical exams. HCH also got us connected with the Canadian Embassy and a wonderful person there who helped us so much in ensuring that we were doing the adoption legally and also applying for the proper visas, residency, citizenship for our soon to be adopted children. The biggest concern of ours was that the adoptions were legal and we could get them their Canadian citizenship quickly. God was so good and helped prepare the way for so much of this for us.

One thing that, from our knowledge, all parents applying to adopt need is a home study. Home studies are an in depth look into the lives of both parents and their home life. This must be done in the home of the parents and cannot be done long distance. It also has to be done by a licensed social worker who is certified to do adoption home studies. In the Dominican Republic, there are no Canadian certified social workers to do this for you. We enquired in Canada about how we get the home study done. They told us that we can hire a social worker, pay for their time to do the study which is usually about $5000 plus have to pay all travel and accommodation costs to travel from Canada to the DR to complete the home study. We were looking at close to $7000 just for the home study. We did not have money like this but we knew that God had plan. He had not taken us as far as He had so far to stop us just because of a little thing like money.

In our area in the DR at this time, there were a few other missionaries and one couple, we had become friends with. Dan and Sue were a fun couple. Sue is Canadian and Dan is American. They are a few years older than us, and had two adopted children that they adopted from the United States. One afternoon, we were having coffee and talking about how our adoption journey was going so far. We shared about trying to get a home study done and what it was going to cost us to get a certified social worker to come and do the home study for us. Dan and Sue looked at each other, in that way that a married couple does when they know something between themselves and smiled. Dan then said that he cd do the home study for us. Paul and I looked at each other, then at Dan, and our mouth opened. We did not speak for a moment and then asked, how? We knew that Dan and Sue did social work in the USA and Canada but, like so many of us missionaries, when God calls us to long term, overseas missions, we tend to let our certificated expire. Dan then shared that even though he has never needed it in their many years in the DR, he never left his certifications expire. He just always felt God telling him to keep them active. Dan was certified and licensed to do adoption home studies. WOW God is so amazing!!!

Over the next couple weeks, Dan visited us in our home and completed the entire, legal adoption home study for us. When we offered to pay him something for his time, at the very least, the supplies (20-page report), he refused. He said that it was his contribution to helping us start our family. We were speechless.

It took us almost six months to compile all the documents that we needed to send over to Haiti to start the adoption process. HCH will not assign a child to adoptive parents until they have received all the documents, and filed with the Haitian government. This made perfect sense to us as why get everyone's hopes up, hearth string attached if it takes years to get documents together and/or the Haitian government will not accept to even look at the petition for adoption.

Getting our documents to HCH was going to be a challenge. Both the Dominican Republic and Haiti have very unreliable mail services. We could not afford to have our documents lost in transit. We contacted Federal Express and UPS to enquire about couriering them from the DR to Haiti. You would think that it would not be too complicated as the two countries are on the same island. Nope - it is complicated. All items sent through FedEx or UPS are sent from the DR to the USA and then to Haiti. The cost for the international courier was very expensive. I cannot remember exactly what it was going to cost but it was something like $200 just to send paper and would take up to three weeks.

We use a private mail service to bring in and take out our mail from the DR called *Missionary Flights International (MFI)*. MFI also services missionaries in the Bahamas and Haiti. I contacted MFI and asked if it would be possible to use them to get our documents to HCH. MFI informed me that HCH was a client of their and because we were both clients, it was possible. I would send our package out on the mail plane on a Tuesday and it would be delivered to Haiti for HCH to pick up on the Thursday. WOW. MFI charges for their services based on the weight of package but at only $0.75 per pound, it was super cheap to send this package via MFI to HCH. I explained to MFI what was in the package and how important it was. MFI not only handled it the package with extreme care, having the pilots carry the package in their "pilot mail bag" rather than putting it in the regular mail bags, they also did not charge us anything to carry the package of documents out of the DR, to the US and then into Haiti. Such a huge blessing.

Two weeks after HCH received our documents, May 2001, they called us asking us if we wanted to adopt a boy or a girl and how old would we like. We had never been to HCH to see any of the children in the orphanage and we trusted that God already had our child chosen. We asked HCH to tell us about their youngest child. We were told that their youngest child is a 9-month old boy who had been in the orphanage for three months. His was healthy. His mother had died and his father could not care for him alone. We said that that is the child that we want!

The process for completing a legal adoption takes time. There are many steps that include social services, lawyers and courts. We were so blessed that we did not have any difficulties but we still had to go through all the steps. As Christmas was nearing, the orphanage contacted us and said that they discovered that they could obtain a visa to the Dominican Republic and legal guardianship for us to bring Noah home while we waited out the adoption process. We were so excited that words cannot describe how we felt.

The man who works for the orphanage (Pierre) to do all the running around for adoption paperwork and legal work went to Port-au-Prince to get a passport, Dominican visa and guardianship papers. All things are a process and take time. Near the end of November, the orphanage called to say that everything had been approved, Pierre, just had to go to Port-au-Prince the following week to pick up the passport with the visa in it. They already had the legal guardianship papers. They expected to be able to bring Noah to us the first week of December.

Early in the first week of December, Pierre went to Port-au-Prince to pick up Noah's passport and visa. Upon entering the downtown area of the city where the Embassy and government buildings are located, he started to hear gun fire. As you got closer, he heard more gunfire and saw people running away from the city core. Pierre quickly learned that a violent coup was being attempted. Pierre turned around and left Port-au-Prince. Later that night, we received a phone call from the orphanage saying what had happened and until things settled down in Port-au-Prince, no one knew when it would be safe to return to Port-au-Prince to pick up Noah's passport and visa.

As disappointed as we were that Noah's documents could not be picked up, we were thankful that Pierre was okay. The days slowly ticked by as we watched the news coming out of Haiti. It took quite for days for things to settle down in Port-au-Prince. The end result was that the coup attempt was unsuccessful but it would be time before Port-au-Prince would be safe.

At about 9 am on December 24, 2001, our phone rang. It was the orphanage. They said that they were successful in getting the passport and visa the day before and Pierre was about to leave the orphanage to drive to the Dominican/Haitian border with Noah. Can we go to the border right away? We were speechless for a moment and then quickly said "YES". However, Pierre would get to the border before we would as he was closer. We were a seven hour drive away. The border is open only from 7 am to 7 pm. Wherever you are come 7 pm, that is where you stay for the night. It was also public market day, which made it easier for Haitians to be at the border towns. We needed to get to the border no later than 5 pm. We had an

67

unreliable vehicle for such a drive but missionary friends had recently been blessed with a new four door truck. They very willingly lent us their truck for this trip. We jumped in the truck and took off for the seven-hour drive to the border.

We arrived safely at the border just before 4 pm. We had no idea what our son looked like or what Pierre looked like. Internet was still a new thing and certainly not fast enough to send photos and we had never seen a photo of our son. At the border town on market day, there are hundreds of Haitians with babies and small children, all trying to sell their goods to make enough money to buy food for their families. We parked, found the town park and started to look around in circles. Within minutes of reaching the town park, a tall Haitian man, carrying a toddler approached us and said "Paul? Sharyn?" I guess that as the only while people in the park, we were easier to spot than it was for us to spot Pierre. Pierre held out Noah to me and handed me my son! Then he said that in the hurry, they forgot the guardianship papers, passport and visa. At this moment, with Noah in my arms, we did not care. We gave Pierre $100 for his border fees and gas, Pierre hugged us, hugged Noah and left. From arriving at the park to walking out of the park, about ten minutes had passed.

We got to the truck, buckled Noah into the car seat, gave him a teddy bear that we had brought for him to cuddle and drove away from the border, heading home. Now a family of three!

"*As for me, I will call upon God and the Lord shall save me.*"

Psalm 55:16

April 2001

Machete Man

It is April and we are working with Medical Ministry International (MMI) as part of the local team leading a surgical medical project in a poor, coastal town called Sabana de la Mar. We are there for two weeks during what is called "Semana Santa"; which means "Holy Week" and is the week before Easter. During Semana Santa, there is a lot of drinking and partying that takes place all over the country and Sabana de la Mar is no different.

We are working at the public hospital, using their facilities to do medical consults, pre-op, surgeries and post-op for our patients. The conditions at the public hospital are not the best but we are blessed that MMI has all their own equipment and that each team brings down so much medical supplies and medication that we usually do not lack for what we need.

One day, I was working upstairs at the hospital preparing various items for the post-op patients that we would have that day when the director of the public hospital comes running up to ask in a panic, asking for help down in the ER. We look around and my boss tells me to go and see what is going on. As I have an emergency background, I was not worried about what I would encounter. As we race downstairs to the ER, the director is telling me that they have a very critical patient who has come into the ER and they do not have the equipment or know what to do to help him. As we turn the corner to enter the ER and I start to put on gloves, I take a quick look at the situation. There are multiple people standing about in a small area, the door outside is wide open with an ambulance outside the door, there is a man on the gurney, a cabinet that is basically empty, a blood pressure cuff on the wall, a nurse standing beside the doctor who is trying to put a stitch into the patient's scalp. Blood is pooling on the floor as the patient is bleeding is profusely from various places.

I approach the doctor and the patient to assess the injuries. The doctor mutters that the patient was attacked by a man with a machete. I can smell alcohol coming from the patient as well as the rusty smell of blood. The doctor whispered that he does not know where to start to control the bleeding. I lean over and start to examine the patient. I observe that he has a large cut down his sternum, large cuts on both forearms, one across his back and one on his head. The cut on his head seemed like the attacker had taken the machete and sliced directly on top of the patient's head. The cut went from the right ear, across the head and down the left side of the head, past the ear to the neck. The cut was so deep that the patient's cerebral was exposed. It just missed the carotid artery. We needed to get the bleeding controlled quickly or this man was going to bleed out and die right there.

I asked the nurse to gather gauze, more gloves, sutures, plasma, iv, tape....... before I could finish, she interrupted to say that they had no supplies at all in the hospital. No wonder the local doctor was so flustered. How do you save a man in this state with no supplies at all? Paul and one of our Dominican staff had come downstairs with the director and I. I called to them both and told them to run upstairs to our supplies and told them what to bring me asap. Within seconds, some of our MMI staff and team members were running back and forth from the ER to upstairs and back. Within about ten minutes, we were able to get all the wounds packed except for the head; which was the largest wound. The nurse had put in two IVs by now but there was no plasma in Sabana de la Mar. This man had lost so much blood and he needed plasma if he was to have any chance of survival. He also needed surgery to close up this major wounds. I went upstairs to our MMI surgical team to talk the case over with the head surgeon. We all agreed that surgery was needed but in order for us to do the surgery, it would take all our staff, all our supplies, all our time, we would have to cancel the surgeries scheduled for the afternoon and we still did not have any plasma. We decided that it would be best to send the patient down to the Capital city where there was plasma and they could operate on him there.

I returned to the ER to speak to the Director and to the patient's family. I explained our decision, why we made the decision as we did and that we needed to get the patient transported to the Capital immediately. The ambulance was still outside and the driver was in the ER watching. The director took over making all the arrangements to get the patient transported while I secured him for transport.

Ambulance workers in the DR are not well trained so I called over the two ambulance workers to give them very specific instructions as to what to do enroute to keep the patient stable, monitor his vitals, and what to do if the patient took a turn for the worse. From the time that I had arrived at the ER until the time that we loaded the patient into the ambulance for transport, about ninety minutes had passed.

We received word about two hours later that they had stopped in San Pedro, which is about one hour from the Capital and were able to get a bag of plasma and start that on the patient while they continued to the Capital.

About three hours later, I was doing evening rounds in the post-op, checking on patients for the final time before calling it quits for the day. One of our Dominican staff came up to me and said, "Tome tu medicina." and handed me an icy cold coke cola. Our staff loves to joke around and because I do not drink coffee but rather coke, they had come to nickname it "tu medicina" (your medicine) and when they would see me starting to fad, would quite often go find me a cold coke without me even asking. This was one of those moments. He put his arm over my shoulder, handed me the cold coke and had a look in his eyes. I looked at him and said "what is it?"

"We just heard from the Capital. Your patient died about thirty minutes ago. You did everything that anyone could have done. If you were not there, he would not have even survived to leave here." Then he hugged me. We were right there in the middle of one of the post-op rooms with the patients looking on. They had, of course, heard about this patient as word travels very fast in this culture. Everyone was quiet as they watched us.

"Thank you for telling me", I said. "I need to finish checking on the other patients then I will be over." I said. At the back of the public hospital, there is an adjoining building that we were all staying in for the two weeks that we were working in Sabana de la Mar.

When I finished rounds about thirty minutes later, I headed back to dorm building to call it a night. As I approached the dining room area, I could hear many voices which was odd at this hour. Usually at this hour, only a few of us would still be up and about as it was always an early start with breakfast at 6:30am. When I walked into the room, everyone stopped talking and turned - I just looked at them wondering what was going on. Then someone, I can not even remember who, said that they heard from the Capital. I was about the cut them off and say that I knew but something stopped me from speaking. They continued to say that there was a mis-communication - our patient had not died! He had been operated on and was recovering in post-op. It was too early to know if there would be any brain damage from the massive cut to his head but he was alive and breathing on his own. Praise God!!!!

The following year, we returned to Sabana de la Mar for another two weeks to do another medical project with MMI. One day as I was working, I can not even remember exactly what I was doing, two people and the director of the hospital came walking up to me. I knew the director but did not know the two people with him. They stopped in front of me and the man embraced me. I was a little dumbfounded as I looked past the man to the director. The director then made introductions.

"This is the man that you treated last year in the ER. The man who had all the machete injuries." My mouth hit the ground.

This man was walking, talking, and very much alive. He then proceeded to tell me that he did have some minimal brain damage and that it sometimes takes him a little bit longer than it use to find the words that he wanted to say but that he was healthy, alive, able to work and provide for his family. He also told met that he goes to church, reads his Bible every day and thanks God every day for his life.

I had often thought about this man during that year and wondered exactly what had happened to him. I can never praise God enough for saving this man's life.

"Come, be my disciples, and I will show you how to fish for people."

Matthew 4:19

2001 – 2004

Dirt to Concrete

In 2001, we started to work in the village of Pedregal, just outside of the town of Jarabacoa in the Dominican Republic. Before doing anything, we wanted to see what were the needs of the local people. We felt God asking us to open a medical clinic and help with the housing in the village. We spent some time just walking through the village, meeting people, sitting on their porches talking and looking about. After a short time of opening the clinic and getting to know the villagers, we found that we could prevent a lot of disease and improve the living conditions of many families just by replacing dirt floors with polished concrete floors.

Many families were living in homes with dirt floors. They would sweep the dirt every day and keep their house clean, however, how clean can you keep dirt? You would be amazed at how clean they did keep the dirt! Living in dirt produces many diseases from parasites that enter the body through the bottom of the foot to fungus, skin diseases and intestinal problems. When it rains, there is nothing but mud and puddles inside of a home with a dirt floor.

In order to start working on replacing the dirt floors in the village with concrete, there were some things that we needed to do first. We had to determine which homes had dirt floors and who wanted concrete floors. We were not going to tell the people that they had to have a concrete floor, however, we did want to help those who wanted a concrete floor. We had to raise funds and we needed some mission teams to come to the country to help out. It was determined that if we could get about five to six teams a year to help with the floors, we could continue to work on the floors between teams. As we began this project, we did not know how many floors were needed to be done in the village but we were committed to make the change.

The first mission team arrived and we explained what the ministry construction projects would be. With the size of the team, Paul figured that we would be able to do three floors in the time that the team would be with us. When we explained about improving the health and living conditions of the families, the team was excited. They worked so hard and completed four floors in eight days!

In a year's time, we had four more teams, and were able to complete 28 floors that first year. However, we were not done. We prayed for more teams to come, more economic resources and we kept pressing forward. We did not have a timetable as to when we wanted to completed this floor project. We would be completed once everyone who wanted a concrete floor had one! The more floors that we did, the more families signed up for a concrete floor.

With the teams and the funds that God provided, we continued to work year round on replacing dirt floors with concrete floors. Each year, we did more floors than the year before. Just over three years after we completed the first floor, we completed the last floor in the village. Everyone who wanted a concrete floor now had one. It only took us three years.

We actually did not do every concrete floor in the village during those three years. The idea caught on. People saw improvement in health and some people who did not want to wait for us to get to their turn, saved up and did their own floors. We were thrilled to see this and always helped out when we could - whether it was with loaning some tools, a day's labour, donating a bag of concrete, or buying the tint for the colouring of the concrete polish. We were just so thrilled to see people taking their own initiative and making an improvement on their own homes and health.

In those three years, and the following couple years, we saw a remarkable improvement on the health of the villagers. We still treated parasites at the clinic but less people had problems with parasites; especially the parasite that enters the body through the bottom of the foot and lives in the dirt. We saw an improvement in skin fungus and other skin diseases, as well as, an improvement in intestinal diseases.

We praise God every time we walk through the village and see a concrete floor. It does not matter if we did the floor or not. Just the fact that there are no more dirt floors in the village, parasite infections are down, and health is improved makes it worth it.

What makes us even more excited as we remember those three years is the number of people that we met, the relationships that we developed, friends that we made and that we were able to share God's love in practical ways to so many families. While mixing concrete side by side with families, we were able to show God's love in action, and to teach about God and His word with our mouths. We did not keep track of numbers but many people asked Jesus into their hearts during our days of mixing and pouring concrete. We were then able to introduce them to a local pastor and help get them plugged into a local church that they could attend and grow in our Lord. This is the real reason why we spent three years pouring concrete floors.

November 2002

Excerpt from Our Newsletter

The Forgotten People

There are thousands of Haitians working and living in the Dominican Republic. They are here to work the sugar cane fields, the DR's number one export. Dominicans do not work the cane fields as they feel that it is below them. In a 12-hour day, a group of three men can cut tow tons of sugar cane and they paid about $2US per day. Cane work is very hard as the men cut each piece of cane by hand, with a machete.

Last month, we took our medical team to the cane fields for a two-week medical outreach. It broke our hearts to see the condition of these people yet at the same time, we learned so much from them and their incredible faith in God. They have so little and such a hard life yet God is still their focus. Incredible!

One day, we saw a two year old baby who weighed just 4 pounds. She was so malnourished and her family did not know what to do for her. Another day, we saw a five week old baby who was born at six pounds and now weighed four pounds. The family did not have the money to go to the hospital to get the tests to find out why this precious child was dying.

"Holy, holy, holy is the Lord Almighty; the whole earth is full of his glory."

Isaiah 5:15

Spring 2002

Forerunner to Prado

When we were adopted our son (our first child), we owned an old two door Toyota Forerunner. We had been praying for a new vehicle but did not have the funds. About three weeks after Noah (our son) came home to us, Paul left me at home, together with a friend who was visiting from North Carolina and on the mission trip, to drive up the mountain to the Pico Duarte National Park. Some other American friends had been up in the parking, hiking to the peak, and Paul was going to pick them up. The group would be spending the night at our house before returning to the United States. The drive to the national park took about one hour and climbed about 4000 feet. As the road got closer to the park, the road became less like a road and more like an off road path.

Paul made it successfully to the National park camp and picked up our friends. It was now after dark and they were heading down to the mountain to home. They had just started the journey down the mountain when the brakes on our Forerunner failed. Thanks be to God for His protection, Paul was able to safely stop the vehicle and no one was hurt. Now came the challenge to get help. It was after dark. It was before cell phones were available in the DR. Internet was sparse and certainly not available at this elevation and near the park. Paul had to hike quite a distance to find a phone to use. He finally found one and was able to call me. I called a friend who, without hesitation, headed up the mountain to rescue the group. It took many hours and the expected return to our house by about 7 pm turned into 1:00 am but they all arrived safe and sound, albeit very tired.

The next day, Paul bought the parts that he needed, hired a mechanic friend and they went back up the mountain to repair the brakes in the middle of nowhere and drive the vehicle back. It took them all day but they did it and returned home safely.

This was just the latest in repairs on this vehicle. However, we had just paid for an adoption and did not have any savings at all so we could not replace the vehicle.

It really worried our friend from North Carolina that we had this unreliable vehicle with the arrival of our son. A couple weeks after this gentleman returned to his home to the US, he called to say that he felt God telling him to lend us money to replace our vehicle and that we could pay him back, interest free, taking as long as we needed to pay off the loan. We were so shocked and surprised. Our only hurdle was that when we entered full time missions, God told us never to personally go into debt apart from a mortgage. About five days later (and before we had replied to our friend), he called us back and said that God just hit him on the head with a baseball and that he cannot lend us the money for a new vehicle but rather he had to give it to us. He gave us $28,000US. That was enough to buy a two year old Toyota Prado with less than 40,000km and for the first year car insurance. We drove that Prado for over ten years and when we traded it in for a new one, it had almost 300,000km on it.

What a blessing from God! It is so amazing what happens when His children are obedient, brave and follow what they believe God is telling them to do.

February 2003

Opening the Clinic

When God first called us into full time, overseas missions, I felt that my calling was to use my medical knowledge as a route to help the local people and share God's love and Word. In October 2002, God opened the door for us to open a medical clinic in a village in the mountains of the Dominican Republic. We found a small house that God provided for us to rent. God brought everything together and the landlord agreed to rent us the house, in order to use as a clinic, for $20 per month. The house was less than 400 square feet. It had an open area that we could use for a waiting area, and two very small bedrooms that could be used for consult rooms. Paul and two men from North Carolina, who had come to serve for two weeks, helped with rewiring, fixing plumbing, building a bookcase, cabinet for medications and an examination table. What a blessing. This was just one of many amazing things that God did to get the clinic open.

In February 2003, we opened the clinic, starting with about 12 hours a week. As word of the clinic started to get out, patients began to come. One of the main focuses for the clinic was to teach. We felt called to teach not only health education and prevention of diseases, but to teach about God. With every patient, we would ask about their faith and pray with them before they left. We do charge a very small consult fee in order for our patients not expect handouts. However, we do our best to keep a stock of medications at the clinic so that we can give our patients, for free, most of the medications they need to treat what ails them.

Over the next few years, the clinic remained opened less than 20 hours a week. An internist, an optometrist and dentist would come up from the Capital city once a week to see patients and help out the clinic. From the beginning and to this day, the clinic has visiting specialists come to treat patients and share God's love and His Word.

We had a couple goals for the clinic. First and foremost is to evangelize to every patient and family member who walked through the door. Our other goals were to treat them physically and spiritually, educate them in order to prevent diseases, and to reach out to the Haitian community. Haitians living the Dominican Republic have a fear of going to public places as many are in the country illegally and fear being sent back to Haiti. Our goal was to provide a clinic that their medical and spiritual needs could be met without fear.

In late 2004, the number of patients had increased, and, we needed help. We prayed and asked God to send someone who could work at the clinic and for the funds to pay the salary. God sent Ana Maria. Ana Maria had never done any administrative or nursing type work before but she was willing. The best part of Ana Maria is that she is a strong believer and not shy to share about God. As patients are waiting to be seen by a doctor, Ana Maria is preaching the Gospel and evangelizing to them. No one comes to the clinic and does not hear about God from

Ana Maria. And no one left without being prayed for by either the doctor and/or Ana Maria. Hearts were changing and we were seeing people returning to the clinic just for spiritual counseling, prayer or to enjoy the social atmosphere of the clinic. Best of all - we were seeing people ask Jesus into their hearts!

By 2007, we needed a full time doctor. I talked with Ana Maria about this and we started to pray. Then, about a week later, Ana Maria gave me the number of someone that I had never heard of, Wendy, and told me to call her. I discovered that Wendy is a local general medicine doctor, unhappy in her current location and praying for a change. After interviewing and a visit to the clinic, Wendy accepted a full time position with the clinic. We prayed about how to pay Wendy's salary and currently have 55% of her salary being sponsored. Wendy is still the main doctor at the clinic and is in charge of all the medical part of the clinic and we continue to have specialists come. Ana Maria is now the administrator of not only the clinic, but also the ministry in country. God is amazing in who He has sent to the clinic.

Since Wendy started working and ministering at the clinic, the number of patients have more than doubled. She shares the original vision of the clinic and, will not let a patient leave without praying with them. She, like Ana Maria, evangelizes to every patient and helps them out spiritually, as the Lord directs.

In January 2013, the landlord gave us six-month notice that he wanted us to move as he wanted his house back. We did not know what we were going to and started to pray. God provided us another house to rent and convert into a clinic. This house is about 150 m down the dirt, village road from the old clinic location. It is about 900 square feet with three rooms so we now have a dedicated pharmacy, a kitchen area and another room that is now our ministry office. The property is quite large and we have been able to plant a ministry garden which produces food that we give away to the poorest of the poor. God is so amazing.

Today, the clinic has a patient load of over 14,000. Patients come from near and far to the clinic. We have continued to reach out to the Haitian community and now, about 30% of our patient load are Haitians. In the past couple of years, we have seen an increase in our Haitian patients. When the patients would register and give their personal information, we were learning that entire families are now coming all the way from Haiti; paying transport and taking days to travel, just to come to our clinic. We are all very humbled by this! We are all working hard to ensure that we always have enough medication on hand to treat the needs of the family so that they can return home to Haiti with a consult, medications, hearing the gospel and being prayed for.

The clinic has become a social point, not only in this village, but in the surrounding areas. People come to be seen by our doctors, as well as, to hang out for an hour or two; hearing the Word, talking about God, or sharing about their lives with others in order to receive advice, help and prayer. We do not treat just the physical, but also the spiritual needs of everyone who comes to the clinic. This is God's clinic and we thank God every day for using us in this manner to share God's love with every person that God sends to the clinic.

In the summer of 2015, the landlord approached us with an offer to purchase the land and property. We agreed upon a purchase price that is approximately $55,000. The landlord transferred the land title into our ministry name right away and has given us 18 months to pay for the land. It is such a blessing from God and we are so thankful to have our land for the ministry.

"Not by might nor by power, but by my Spirit says the Lord Almighty."

Zechariah 4:6b

2003

Elena

My first patient who came to the clinic when I opened our doors on 23 February 2003 was a 35 year old lady who was complaining of abdominal pains. She explained that she has had these pains for a long time.

"What is a long time", I asked.

She responded, "Oh, about a year."

"Have you been to any other doctors for treatment?"

"Yes, they said it was gastritis but it is getting worse. The medicine does not help at all."

"Okay, well let's get you examined and runs some tests.

I sent her for urine and blood work as well as an abdominal sonogram. My sponsored doctor was coming on Friday so I asked the patient to return Friday with her test results.

Come Friday, our patient returned with her test results. Dr. Abreu looked over the results with me and we both saw that the sonogram showed a growth of some sort in her uterus. We were suspecting a uterine tumour. We referred her a gynecology surgeon in the closest city for a consult to have the growth removed. The next few weeks had outpatient making multiple trips to the city for consultations with the surgeon, repeat lab work and repeat sonograms. The surgeon scheduled surgery for a Tuesday morning to remove the growth and send it for biopsy.

On the Monday afternoon, our patient headed to the clinic in the city to have a final sonogram and lab work before her surgery in the morning. The surgeon came by to talk with the patient Monday evening. He concurred that the sonogram earlier that afternoon showed the growth to still be in her uterus, still growing and now appeared to be about the size of a tennis ball. Time to get it removed. We were all suspecting that the biopsy would show it to be malignant - cancerous.

Our patient is the wife of a local pastor with a strong faith. Not only was she praying but so were her entire church, family, friends, other churches as well as those in our ministry. We were asking for a miracle to happen. Our patient had a couple young children at home, is a wonderful lady, a woman of God, a supporter to many, and a prayer warrior with God at the centre of her life.

Early Tuesday morning, our patient is taken to the ER and prepped for surgery. The anesthesiologist administers and monitors the medication as our patient is put to sleep. The surgeon re-examines the latest sonogram to confirm the location of the tumour then began the surgery. Our patient's husband, family and friends are all waiting and praying while the surgery takes place.

Just over an hour later, the surgeon comes to our patient's room to speak with her and her family about the results of the surgery. As the surgeon enters the room, the family cannot make out if the look on his face is one of joy or sadness but more like confusion. The surgeon begins by saying that he cannot really explain what he found when he did the surgery. "I have never seen anything like this before and I cannot explain it. I know that we were right to operate, you have six sonograms over the past month that all show the tumour and the continued growth of the tumour. However, when I opened your uterus to remove the tumour, there was nothing! Your uterus was healthy and there was no mass! I just cannot explain it."

The family started to cry and scream out praises to God. "Thank you God for healing. You are the Great Physician!". God had chosen to heal our patient! There was no tumour, no cancer. Thirteen years later, our patient is still our patient and has not had any recurrence of any tumour anywhere in her body. She has had no major health problems since the day of that surgery back in 2003. She continues to serve at her husband's side as he pastors a local church. Her children are growing and she is enjoying her granddaughter now. She is still a huge prayer warrior and works with the ladies and children in her church.

Thank you again, God our Physician, for choosing to heal this child of yours so that she could continue to serve you here on earth!

It has been amazing to watch God heal people, as this patient is not our only patient that we have witnessed His divine healing and the only explanation that we can give is to Praise God for his healings. Not all our patients receive healing. It is God's choosing, not ours. It has been an honour to witness the healings that God has chosen to perform through our clinic.

March 2003

Excerpt from Our Newsletters

Everyone Needs the Lord

On our medical teams, we have all sorts of people who come to serve and work with us from all kinds of backgrounds. On our last medical project at the end of January, we had a young man join us who is a medical student. He has Christian friends back home but does not know the Lord and has been thinking a lot about the Lord Jesus and "all that Christian stuff". During the first week of the project, many of the younger people on the team had had opportunities to share their stories and their faith with him. On the Sunday, when the team went to a local church service, the topic was all about making your decisions and this young man really felt like there was no one else there and the sermon was being spoken directly to him. After returning to the camp, he called his fiancée back home, spent some time with the Lord and then came to share his news. Paul and I were honoured to be two of the first people that he told that he had made the decision to follow the Lord and dedicated his life to God. Praise God!!!

"Religion that God our Father accepts as pure and faultless is this: to look after orphans and widows in their distress and to keep oneself from being polluted by the world."

James 1:27

August 2003 – June 2010

Patrisio

I exited my office to see an older gentleman waiting in to be seen. On first appearance, he had poor hygiene, dirty clothes, obviously poor, smelt of body order, smoke and alcohol and held onto a stick he used as a cane to help him walk. I smiled at him as I proceeded to my secretary to give the file that I just completed. My secretary handed me a new file and introduced me to Patrisio.

He stood up, on shaky legs, shook my hand and followed me into the office. Patrisio explained his medical issues to me, we talked about his history and lifestyle. He was a hard man who had had a hard life. He was now 73 years old and told me that he had a dozen children but not one of them lived near or visited. We talked a bit about God but he was very closed to this topic. We gave him some medications for his various problems and asked him to return in a week to check up on him.

Exactly one week later, in walks Patrisio. I have to admit that I was a bit surprised. I did not think that he would do anything that we suggested in regards to his medical care, let alone come back in a week. After speaking with him, we learned that he did everything that we had asked, except a change in diet. He was happy with feeling a bit better and stronger already. However, he still was not the least bit interested in talking about God.

Ana Maria, my secretary, has a natural, evangelistic heart and talks about God to every person who walks into the clinic. After Patrisio left on his second visit, Ana Maria and I talked a bit about him and how closed he was to God. Ana Maria shared that Patrisio has lived in the village longer than she has been alive and he is a hard man. He did not have a good reputation and no one was surprised that his family did not come often to visit him. This all made me sad.

Over the next seven years, Patrisio continued to come in for his monthly checks, get his medications for the month and visit. It seemed that each time he came, he hung out a bit longer just to visit. We all sensed that he was a lonely man. We started to look forward to the times that Patrisio would come to the clinic. When I would see him walking towards the clinic door, it would put a smile on my face. Over the years, friendship developed but Patrisio remained very closed to God, although we never gave up sharing about God, praying with him (which he always allowed us to do) and praying for him.

After about seven years, on one of Patrisio's monthly visits to the clinic, he had a new complaint. A pain and other symptoms that instantly put up the alerts for possible prostate cancer. We sent him down to the city to consult with an urologist and asked him to return to us with the results of the consult with the urologist.

We learned years earlier that Patrisio had never learned to read and he lived alone so there was no one at home to read things for him. Sometimes, he would bring things to us to ask us to read them for him. This day when he came, he brought a young man with him and the report from the urologist. Patrisio introduced the young man as his son who was visiting from New York. I asked Patrisio if he knew what the results said even before I read them. He said that the urologist said that he had an infection. The son asked to speak to me privately before I spoke with Patrisio so we proceeded into the office.

I started to read the report while the son took a seat in the office. Tests showed a positive result for prostate cancer. The son started to talk and shared that they were telling Patrisio that he has a urinary infection so he needs the medication (pain killers and antibiotics) to treat that and asked me to not tell Patrisio that he has cancer. I looked at the son and said that I could not do that. Not only is it dishonest, it is wrong. A patient has the right to know what is wrong with him and to make his own decisions about treatment. There was nothing wrong with Patrisio's mind and, as sad as the results are, he needs to know the truth. I told the son that he can tell Patrisio or I will. The son said that he could not tell him, can I tell him?

We called Patrisio into the office and I explained the results of the tests from the urologist. Patrisio looked at his son and at me, and said that he knew that it was more than infection. He was so glad to finally know what was wrong with him. We explained his options, including surgery. By this time, Patrisio was 80 years old. He said that he did not want surgery or chemo. He will take medications and would be grateful if we would help him out with managing the pain but no surgery or chemo. It was a tearful time as Patrisio's son cried as he heard his father's decisions but he did support them. Then Patrisio asked Ana Maria and I to pray for him and his family. It was the first time he had asked for prayer.

The urologist predicted that Patrisio would have about 12 to 18 months to live without treatment. Patrisio's son had to return to New York but he did come back to visit his Dad every four to six months after that which brought a lot of joy to Patrisio.

As I have mentioned, Patrisio was a hard, stubborn man and he decided that he was not going anywhere just yet. Patrisio continued to come to our clinic every couple of weeks for the next four years until he started to get really sick. When Patrisio started to get really sick, he got sick quickly. Within a few weeks, he was unable to get out of bed and was in a lot of pain. By this time, Dra. Wendy had joined our clinic staff and had taken over Patrisio's treatment a couple years earlier. Once Patrisio could no longer come to the clinic, Ana Maria started to go by Patrisio's house to visit and pray for him about once a week.

I was in Canada visiting churches when one Sunday evening, Ana Maria had someone come running up to her door, calling out for her. "Patrisio wants you to come now! Can you come? He is asking for you." Ana Maria got dressed and went to Patrisio. It was almost 11:00pm.

When Ana Maria got to Patrisio's bedside, he whispered and asked, "Is it too late to be with Jesus?" "Of course not!", replied Ana Maria. "We can pray right now if you wan to?" Patrisio responded saying that he did. Ana Maria started to pray for Patrisio and then Patrisio prayed and asked Jesus to come into his heart and even though his time on earth was almost over, he wanted to live for eternity with God in heaven.

There were many neighbours gathered about, caring for Patrisio in his final days and many from the church were there that night praying for Patrisio. Patrisio told Ana Maria that he knew that one day he would ask Jesus into his heart but that he was such a stubborn man, it took too long but he was so happy and filled with joy as he lay on that bed dying. He thanked Ana Maria for coming as it meant so much to him to pray with her and have her near in his final time. Twenty minutes later, God took Patrisio home.

I have often thought of Patrisio over the years; both before he passed away and since. We have all gone through some very hard times in life, made bad decisions and chose to accept or reject God. It is never too late to change our mind and accept God. Patrisio did and when he did pass away, he passed away with a smile on his face and love and joy in his heart. I miss dear Patrisio and praise God that he is now dancing in heaven.

September 2003

Excerpt from Our Newsletters

Small and Mighty

Every year, we take our medical teams to the same areas. Last year, we went to *El Arroyo* and I had a patient who was just weeks old, Liza. Liza was born at 7lb 4 oz. but at four weeks old, she weighed only 4 pounds. Her Mom did not know why her baby was so sick and she was doing all that she knew to so. Liza's Mom is a good Mom but lacked resources, knowledge and money. I spent about an hour with Liza and her Mom last year; examining Liza, educating Mom and doing all that we could. I told Mom to take Liza to the local clinic and weigh her every day to ensure that she was gaining until Liza weighed 10 pounds. When we left El Arroyo that day, I was not convinced that little Liza would be alive four weeks later.

This year, we returned to El Arroyo with the medical team. In the busyness of this 70 person medical team, I had forgotten that we were going to Liza's village. We had been at El Arroyo about two hours when a young mom left the line up, pushed her way into the gates and came straight to me. She pushed a baby girl into my arms who was about a year old and started to say "gracias gracias". She asked me if I remembered her and her dying baby from last year. Right away, I clicked into who this mom was and felt a tear in my eye. Here I was holding little Liza - weighing in at a healthy 21 pounds and just as health as any other one year old baby girl. Miracles do happen and God is in Control!!!

May 2003

Citizenship Arrived Just in Time

God does know what is about to happen and is preparing the way even when we do not know it. One example of God preparing the way before we knew it was in May 2003.

In November 2002, we had been able to take Noah, our son we adopted from Haiti, to Canada under his residency application. As soon as we landed in Toronto, Noah was awarded his residency visa. In order to obtain Noah's Canadian citizenship, we had to apply for it and wait through the process. It was automatic that Noah would receive Canadian citizenship but we still had to go through the process. In November 2002, we were able to visit most family members and introduce them to Noah. What a blessing and joyous trip that was. Then, we return to our ministry work and home in the Dominican Republic.

Part of the citizenship process is that once the application has been accepted, you have turn in your residency card and await your citizenship card. During this period of time, you cannot travel in or out of Canada. Wherever you are when you turn in the residency card is where you stay until you receive your citizenship card. We received notice in late March 2003 that Noah's citizenship application was accepted and immigration was requesting us to turn in Noah's residency card so that his citizenship card could be issued. Immigration informed us that it usually takes about 12 weeks before we would receive the citizenship card. As we had no immediate plans to fly to Canada, we felt that it was a good time to turn in the residency card so we mailed it to Canadian Immigration.

In the Dominican Republic, we receive mail twice a month via a private mail service called Missionary Flights International (MFI). MFI brings in and takes out missionaries' mail for various Caribbean countries. With the slower method of receiving our mail, we expected to receive Noah's citizenship card in about July. We mailed the residency card at the beginning of April.

Exactly four weeks from the day that we mailed out the residency card, we received mail via MFI. In our mail was an envelope from Canadian Immigration. It was Tuesday 9 May 2003. Instantly, we thought that there was a problem with the citizenship as there was no way that Noah's citizenship card would have arrived already. We opened the envelope and literally, caught our breath as Noah's citizenship card dropped into our hands. How could this be. How could we have Noah's Canadian citizenship and his card within four short weeks. We were ecstatic. Voices elevated, hugging and praising God. What a miracle! Praise God!!

A couple hours later, Paul called his parents in Victoria BC to share the exciting news. Paul's Mom had helped us out with various things during the application process and we knew that she would be thrilled to hear this great news. As expected, Mom and Dad were both thrilled. Even though we had no plans to fly to Canada right away, just knowing that we could whenever we wanted to or needed to gave us so much peace. Thank you God!

"We always thank God the Father of our Lord Jesus Christ when we pray for you."

Colossians 1:3

December 2003 – January 2004

Small Packages

At the beginning of January, a young girl names Juli came knocking on my door on a Saturday and asked if I could come to her sister's home to help her sister's baby. Juli said that it was urgent, that the baby was dying. At the time, I had no idea what Juli was talking about but I went to the home and met Liliana (only 17 yrs. old) and her son Cristian. Cristian was born prematurely on December 4, 2003 weighing only one pound and with a fight in him for survival. Cristian was released four weeks later, still weighing one pound and with a severe infection on his foot. The infection was caused by the IV that the hospital put in. Cristian was so tiny that the only place that they could put an IV in was his foot. The hospital staff then left the IV in his foot for four weeks, never changing it or cleansing it. It got severely infected. The hospital staff did not remove the IV and it continued to fester. Liliana was not breast feeding as the local doctor told her that because she gave birth too early, her milk is bad. Cristian had not had any breast milk – only powdered milk because that was all that Liliana could afford. As Liliana never breast fed, her milk dried all up by the time that I met Liliana.

I assessed Liliana and Cristian and was very sad by what I saw. This little, itty baby was dying. The infection on his foot was life threatening, he had not gained any weight in his four short weeks of life, he was lethargic, unresponsive and not breathing well. Lilian was so scared, exhausted and could hardly put two thoughts together. She looked to Juli for the answer to every question that I asked. After spending about thirty minutes with the family, I said that I had to go home to make a phone call and would return in a bit.

I have a friend who had just retired after many years as a neo-natal specialist in upper state New York. I called Bill right away. I explained the situation and Cristian's case to Bill and asked him for help. I had no clue what medicine to administer or at what dosages. With Cristian weighing only one pound, the dosage of any medication had to be exact or the medicine could kill Cristian. Bill's heart broke after hearing about Cristian. He was unable to jump on a plane but he was willing and able to be the specialist by proxy. Bill prescribed medication and gave me the exact dosages. Paul and I went to the clinic to the get the medication as well as buy some highly nutritional milk that would help with healing and growing for Cristian. What Cristian really needed though was breast milk.

We returned to Liliana's home. I sat down with Liliana, her husband, and Juli and explained everything that Bill and I had talked about. I explained to them that we were going to do our very best to help them but that Cristian's survival was very must in God's hands and we would not make any guarantees. I told them that they would have to follow our instruction exactly as we said and they agreed. I explained what medication we wanted to give Cristian and why. For now, the only medication that we were giving him was an antibiotic for the infection on his foot. I then showed Liliana, her husband and Juli how to property clean Cristian's foot and the infection and how often.

I showed them the milk that we had bought and how to prepare it for Cristian. I told them that breast milk would be the very best as there is nothing that man has made that can duplicate the health benefits of a mother's milk. Juli then said that she had given birth to her daughter about a month before Cristian was born and that she was breast feeding. Juli said that if it would be okay and not make Cristian sick, she would be willing to breast feed her daughter as well as Cristian. Liliana was okay with this idea so it was agreed that Juli would try and see if she had enough milk.

I would check on Liliana and Cristian every day. For the first week, every day I was surprised that I did not get the call that Cristian had passed away but Cristian is a fighter and survivor and he has been his whole life. Juli was producing enough milk to feed her daughter and Cristian, however, it was not always convenient. I was able to get a breast pump, show Juli how to use it and she was able to pump her milk so that Lilian could have bottle of milk available for when Cristian was hungry – especially in the middle of the night. Neither Juli nor Lilian owned a fridge but the "corner" store had a fridge and electricity. They agreed to let Juli and Lilian keep a few bottles of milk in their fridge so that the milk would not go bad. This allowed Juli to pump milk and be able to leave her home to do what she needed to do and still have milk for Cristian. It also made the night easier on both Juli and Liliana as Liliana did not need to wake Juli if Cristian woke in the night hungry.

Every day for the first few weeks, Bill and I would talk on the phone to go over Cristian's progress. Bill would change the dosages of the medications as Cristian would gain an ounce, and then another ounce, then another, etc. Bill added a vitamin to the medication. After about a month, the infection on Cristian's foot was finally gone and we were able to stop the antibiotic. Cristian was healing and gaining weight. As Cristian got healthier, his attention grew, became more interactive and gained some energy. He was becoming a typical baby.

After about two months, our daily consults dropped to every other day, then every three days, then two times a week, then once a week. After about six months, Cristian weighed 3 pounds and 8 ounces! It took God's miracle and the help of the village to bring Cristian to good health and we praise God for Cristian's healing!!!

Today, Cristian is 12 years old, a little small for his age but physically healthy. Due to being born so premature, he is developmentally impaired and slow to learn. Through our ministry, he has someone who is sponsoring him so that he can attend a special needs schools in the area operated but another ministry. He is smart and quickly learning many things.

God is good, amazing and loves His children. We so clearly see this in Cristian's life!

May 9, 2003

What we did not know, but what God knew was what the next few days would hold for us all.

On Thursday evening, our phone rang. It was one of Paul's sister and the instant that Paul answered, he could tell from the tone of voice that something was wrong. Paul's sister told us that Mom and Dad had gone out for dinner and Mom had a major heart attack. She was at the hospital but had not regained consciousness. Paul's sister does not live in Victoria so the two were able to talk and comfort each other as neither were in Victoria. When Paul hung up, he called his family in Victoria right away. He talked with his brother and another sister who were at the hospital. I cannot remember if Paul talked with his Dad or not. The report was that it was a major heart attack, Mom had not gained consciousness and the doctors were not very optimistic. There were numerous phone calls that went back and forth during the night. Paul's Dad said that it would be okay and not to fly home but we were talking and praying about just that. We decided that at the very least, Paul needed to go to Victoria and needed to get there as soon as possible. We all knew that Mom's condition was very serious.

Paul called his family in the morning and told them that we were going to try to get a flight to Victoria as soon as possible but we did not know when yet. Paul's sister was also calling the airlines to book a flight to fly to Victoria. Everyone was headed home.

As we were getting organized to head to town to our friends who run a travel agency, our phone rang. Paul picked up the phone, listened for a bit then collapsed. I grabbed the phone but I already knew what had been said. Paul's mother opened her eyes while Dad was right there at her bedside. She looked at Dad. Dad said that everything was going to be okay. Sandy and Paul were on their way home to see her. She smiled up at Dad, squeezed his hand and then fell back asleep. Dad was encouraged to go get something to eat now that Mom had woken and was asleep. Dad left the hospital room and no sooner did he leave the room, that Mom passed away.

I hung up the phone and then went to Paul. We held each other and cried. Paul was inconsolable. The miles between the Dominican Republic and Canada never felt so far away as they did at that moment. I picked up the phone and called our good friends, Daniel and Angela who hurried over to the house. In the Dominican culture, when a friend has a family member die, everyone comes over to the house right away. As our friends could not go to Mom's house, so they came to our house. Within about an hour, our house was filling up with dear friends who loved us. Some friends were in the kitchen preparing food and drinks. I was with Paul but I knew that I had to get to the travel agent to get plane tickets. In 2003, we did not have internet in our house in the Dominican Republic and booking tickets online was not as common as it is today.

Daniel and Angela told me to go. Daniel would not leave Paul's side and Angela would care for Noah. Noah was only 2 years and 9 months old. I told Paul where I was going and left for the travel agent's. I arrived at the office and explained to Gloricel and Jose that Paul's Mom had just died and we needed to get to Canada right away. The flights off the island were very limited. There was one a day out of Santiago to the US. Once we got to Miami, we would have to transfer to two more flights and a ferry ride before arriving in Victoria. It would take us about 36 hours from departing Santiago to arriving in Victoria. Gloricel then asked me if I was going or staying with Noah in the DR. It was then that it hit me how God had already prepared the way. Noah had his Canadian citizenship as of three days ago! He could travel without restrictions! We did not have his Canadian passport yet but we had his citizenship and that was all that we needed. PRAISE GOD. HE prepared the way before we even knew it!

As Gloricel and José were finding us flights to Victoria, they also called the airline, which was American Airlines, to ask about bereavement refund. American Airlines said that we will have to pay for the tickets at full fare then apply for a bereavement discount and submit a copy of the death certificate. We were able to obtain flights that would leave first thing in the morning, Saturday 13 May. The total cost of the three tickets was $7000. Our credit card, even though at a zero balance, had a limit of $3000. We could not buy the tickets. We did not have $7000. Gloricel and José immediately said that their agency would buy the tickets under their credit and it would be thirty days before interest was charged to them. If we paid them back in less than 30 days, they would pay for the difference on the tickets. WOW To this day, we have never forgotten what Gloricel and José did for us that day so that we could get to Canada. We thank God and we thank Gloricel and José. We had no idea how we would pay the $7000 but we knew that God had a plan and trusted Him.

The only seats that were available on the plane from Santiago to Miami were in three different locations on the plane. There was no way that we were having our 2 year old sit between two strangers, all alone. Nor, did I want my husband to be alone as he grieved so deeply for his mother. When we got to the airport and checked in, the ticket agent said that she could do nothing to change our seats and we had to ask at the gate. At the gate, they basically said that same thing. They said that we would have to stand at the gate and ask passengers if anyone was will trade seats so that we could sit together. One person agreed so now we had two seats together in the front row of economy. The agent at the gate told us to talk to the flight attendant when we got on board the plane. We proceeded to do this. The flight attendant was great. She completely understands our grief and emotional state. She went to the man who had the third seat in the row where we had two seats and asked him if he would mind switching seats..... to a first class seat. The flight attendant gave a first class seat to this stranger so that we three could sit together. It warmed our hearts after dealing with ticket and gate agents who were not helpful but also were not sympathetic. They increased our stress and difficulty. The flight attendant onboard even brought ice cream for us from first class during the flight. She was wonderful.

We cleared customs and immigration in Miami, connected with the Dallas flight and killed a few hours waiting for the connection. Then, we did the same thing in Dallas as we waited for our connection to Vancouver. Once in Vancouver, my aunt and uncle met us at the airport and took us to their home for the night. It was so good to be around some family after such a hard two days. My aunt and uncle took us to the ferry terminal the next morning where we caught the ferry from Vancouver to Victoria. Upon arriving in Victoria, Paul's family was there to pick us up and Paul was now surrounded by his family during this time of grief.

It was some difficult days as the family talked and made many decisions. Paul and I called our Pastor to tell him that we were in town now. (We had already been in touch with him on the day that Mom had passed away.) Paul's family wanted a funeral but no one attended church except for us. They asked Paul if our pastor would do the funeral. The next day, we went to talk with our pastor; who agreed to do the funeral as well as help in any way possible. The entire church and our church family gathered around the family to love, pray and support in many ways.

On Monday morning, on the advice of Gloricel, I got on the phone to American Airlines right away to apply for the bereavement refund. I needed to find out exactly what we had to do to apply as Gloricel had informed me that there is a strict deadline for this refund. Long story short is that I learned from American Airlines that there would be no bereavement refund. One of the policies of American Airlines for their bereavement refund is that you have to originate or finish your flights in the US in order to obtain the bereavement refund. No one told us that. No one had told Gloricel this either when she called American Airlines to see if our flights would qualify for the bereavement refund. Now, here we were, with a $7000 bill and no bereavement discount from the airlines.

One conversation that our pastor brought up was his curiousity about our airfare. We told him the long story of getting the tickets, Gloricel and José helping to pay for them and American Airlines not giving us any bereavement discount. Our pastor said that the previous Sunday, they had taken a large extra offering so he just could not pass the basket again this coming Sunday. However, he said that he will share our story with the congregation and put a basket at the back of the church if anyone felt lead to help us out with paying for the tickets. We were grateful for this gesture. Our pastor did warn us not to expect much as you can only "go to the well" so often.

At church Sunday morning, the pastor did just as he said that he would. The basket was at the back of church and not passed hand to hand. On Tuesday, the pastor called Paul. He asked if we could drop by the church to pick up the offering that did come in on Sunday to help with our airfare. When we got to the church later that day, the pastor invited us to his office. He then asked us if we had been able to pay for any of the airfare yet. We shared that we had about $800 in our savings that we already applied to our credit card. We also had received a couple donations from friends from other parts of Canada and US to help with airfare that totaled about $2200. We were still short about $4000. The pastor then handed an envelope to Paul and said that the envelope contained the offering from having the basket at the back of the church on Sunday. He waited and asked Paul to open the envelope. When Paul did, he was speechless and handed it to me. I looked and was also speechless. The amount put into the basket at the back of the church was $4000. It was over double what was raised by the church the week earlier. The pastor said that he has never had a Sunday morning extra offering be that large.

$4000 was exactly what we needed to send Gloricel and José to pay off our plane tickets. In less than one week, God had paid for the plane tickets! We knew that God would provide the $7000. We had no idea how or who He would use but we knew that He would provide and He did! It was all God!!!

We spent four weeks in Victoria with Paul's family as we helped Dad and the family with many things that come with a dear family member passing. Paul was also able to spend time with his Dad and all his siblings on various occasions as they grieved together over the sudden loss of Mom. It was a blessed time that God gave us.

"Because you have seen me, you have believed; blessed are those who have not seen and yet have believed."

John 20:29

2004

Best Christmas Presents Ever, Part II

About 18 months after Noah came home, we prayerfully decided to do it all again. It was time to get a sibling for Noah. We reached out to the orphanage to see if it possible to do a second adoption and go directly through them. Not many rules and laws had not changed at all since we adopted Noah. The orphanage reminded us of the documents that we needed and pointed out a few news ones that were now required. We reached out to our friends who did our first home study and discovered that being that it was under five years since our first home study, just a quick visit to the home and an amendment was all that was needed to our home study. This took about one hour in order to complete.

I started the task of gathering documentation again. Some of the documents I already had as I could use the same onesas we used for Noah, like birth and marriage certificates. Some things had to be done again with the current date. It took us about six months to accumulate all the documents and ensure that we everything in both English and French. One thing that I did this time, that I did not do before sending our package of documents to Haiti, was to put them on a scale and weigh them. The final package, with copies of everything in both English and French, actually weight 9 pounds!

Shortly before sending our documents to Haiti, we were talking with the orphanage. As we were ready to send our documents, the orphanage asked us details about a child that we would like to adopt. We asked "who is youngest, female child?". They told us about a toddler who had come into the orphanage at 13 months old and weighed only 14 pounds. She was very malnourished and God healed her. She still had a road to travel to get back to perfect health but she was healthy, and gaining weight. "That is our girl", both Paul and I said.

Two weeks later, late January, early February 2004, we sent over our documents to the orphanage so that the legal process of adopting our daughter could begin. Our papers arrived in Haiti one week before the coup d'état of President Aristide in February 2004. The government fell and for the next three plus years, there was no real, functional government. Once again, we were waiting on the paperwork in order to bring our girl home. For the months following the coup, no one really knew what was going on with the government and those who won the coup. We, like so many in Haiti, had to just wait it and see what would happen.

Our daughter, who we named Samantha, had birth parents who lived close to the orphanage. They are very poor and due to their extreme poverty; they could not feed Samantha. This is why they put her in the orphanage. The orphanage had food and could find her a family who could feed her.

In the fall, with no end in sight for adoption petitions to be processed by the government, the orphanage asked us if we would like to do the same thing that we did with Noah?

Obtain legal guardianship so that Samantha could come home to us while we are waited to see what would happen with the Haitian government. We jumped at this opportunity and said yes! Samantha's birth father agreed to go with Mathieu to Port-au-Prince to apply for a passport and Dominican visa. As the birth father still was the legal guardian of Samantha, only he could sign these legal documents. The orphanage had not been able to complete the sign over of legal guardianship to the orphanage due to the coup. Mathieu and the birth father made numerous trip to Port-au-Prince to obtain a passport, Dominican visa and finally, legal guardianship for Paul and I for Samantha. This was all time consuming to obtain. A few times when Mathieu went to Port-au-Prince, it was too dangerous to enter the city due to riots and such. We were all hoping to have Samantha home in early December but this was not to be due to the times that Mathieu could not enter Port-au-Prince due to the dangers.

At 10 am on December 23, 2004, the orphanage called to say that they had the passport, visa and guardianship paper. We thanked God for the birth father helping as he did to obtain these legal papers. The orphanage asked us if we could go to the border NOW, be there by 4pm, to pick up Samantha. "Of course" was our reply. We called a few friends and family, passed along the news and asked for prayer coverage. We grabbed Noah, a doll that we had bought for Noah to give to Samantha and ran out the door. We left so quickly that we did not have water or even a change of clothing for Noah. Noah was now 4 years old. It would be a long day but we would stop as we passed through the city to buy food and water.

By 2004, more people had cellular phones, including us. However, as you approach the border on either side, there is no cell phone coverage for about 20 km. Companies on either side of the border do not want people stealing cell coverage without plans and payments. As we reached the last good size town before the border, San Juan de la Maguana, I checked our cell phone. No calls or message. Shortly after passing through San Juan, we lost cell coverage. We were a bit late arriving at the park at the border. It was about 4:30pm. When we arrived at the park, we looked for Mathieu and our girl, but saw no one. We have no cell phone service. We went to a corner store, called a "Colmado" and bought a snack for Noah and drinks for us all. Even though it was December 23rd, this is the Caribbean and it was warm. Noah was glad to be out of the jepeta (SUV in Spanish) and we let him run around while we watched and waited. The time ticked on, the sun started to set. Still no Mathieu. Still no Samantha. It is now 6 pm. Still no one. We are all getting anxious. As it gets dark, we are starting to get a little, to be honest, scared. We have no idea why they are no there yet. Noah is getting restless and hungry. I could not eat at all. We found some food for us to eat for dinner and continued to wait.

A few of the local people approached us to ask if we were okay. They had noticed that had been hanging around the park for a long time. The public market was closed. It was dark. The work day was over and people were heading home. It is now 7 pm and the border is closed for the night. We still waited. We just could not bring ourselves to driving away from the border without our daughter. Finally, after 8 pm, we made what we felt was the impossible decision..... We got in our jepeta and drove away from the border. We were all silent. I was glad to see, after about twenty minutes, that Noah had fallen asleep. He was exhausted. Paul and I were in shock.

After about 30 minutes of driving, my phone beeped. We had cell service again. And we had a message waiting. I called in to collect the message. It was the orphanage. They said that Mathieu got a flat tire on the way to the border. By the time that he got to the border, it was 7:05 pm and the border was closed for the night. The message continued to say that Mathieu has family that lives very near the border so they would spend the night there and Mathieu would cross the border at 7 am and meet us at the park. We praised God that they were safe!!! We had not spoken some of our thoughts but both of us had had thoughts of different bad things that could have happened to them on their journey to the border.

We were approaching San Juan de la Maguana and it was 9 pm at night. No time to drive 7 hours home and 7 hours back. What would we do. San Juan did not have a great reputation for being safe. We knew of no safe hotels in the area. We did not know any missionaries in the area. And then we remembered that there is a mission hospital in the area that partners with MMI, the ministry that we were serving with. We called our director, who lives in Santo Domingo. We explained our day! That took a while and then asked if he could give us directions to the mission hospital. It took us about fifteen minutes and we found the mission hospital. By this time, it was getting close to 10 pm. Not a good time to go knocking on people's doors.

There was a watchman at the gate so Paul got out, explained who we were and if we could talk to whoever was in charge of the hospital compound. An American came to the gate, an older gentleman. Paul introduced himself and then briefly told him our situation and that we needed a place to stay the night so that we could return to the border at 7 am and get our daughter. Jay, the American told the watchman to let us in.

Once we were parked, we all got out of the truck. Noah was just exhausted. We had not eaten much, were thirsty and had absolutely nothing for spending the night. No clothing, no toothbrush, nothing. Jay's wife, Susan came out and introduced herself to us and then asked us to follow her. She led us to a guest room that hospital had. The room was clean and prepared to receive 3 guests. I was surprised as there was no way that Susan had time to prepare anything for us in the less than five minutes since we drove up.

Susan told me that they were just getting ready to go to bed when we rang the gate bell. They had been waiting up for some American doctors to arrive but they just got work that the doctors' flights were delayed and they would arrive the next afternoon. The room that we were put in was prepared for the doctors. God knew!! Susan also told me that they usually do not receive many clothing donations but had just received a very large clothing donation (boxes and boxes). They had not sorted through the clothes yet but she remembered seeing a few items on top. She left, then returned with some clothing that we could used to sleep in. Susan also provided us with some food.

After Susan and Jay said good night, Paul and I sat on the bed just amazed at how God had taken care of us. We were safe. In a safe location. Had some food in our bellies, toothbrushes, bed, we were set. Off to sleep we went.

In the morning, we got up and discovered Susan and Jay waiting for us with a hot breakfast prepared. Susan told me to come with her - she had gotten into some of the boxes of clothing and had pulled some clothes that would fit our daughter and son! What a blessing that Susan and Jay were to us for the 9 hours that we spent with them. We will never forget them and how God used them to help and bless us.

At 7 am, we headed off for the border to get our daughter. We got to the border about 40 minutes later and went to the meeting place, the town park. As we walked up the park, we saw Mathieu with our baby girl. The tears were forming. It had been such a long journey and now, here she is!

It all happened so fast and in less than ten minutes, we were pulling away from the border. We stopped at the hospital that we spent the night at and introduced them to our Samantha. They had forever become part of our family story and bringing Samantha home. God had everything planned. He took care of all of us the night before. We were all safe and sheltered and united in the morning.

While driving the seven hours home, it dawned on me that it was Christmas Eve. December 24th. God brought both of our beautiful children home to us on December 24th.... three years apart.

As a result of the coup and non functional government for a few years in Haiti, our adoption petition sat on the desk of the Minister of Social Services, waiting to be reviewed and signed. However, there was no Minister of Social Services. Three years after the coup, a minister was appointed but did not do much. A year later, another minister was appointed. This was in November 2007 and this new Minister of Social Services made approval of adoption petitions a top priority. From what we were told, she started at the bottom of the pile, addressing the oldest petitions first. Our petition for adoption was the second petition approved by the new Minister. She approved it and passed it on to the courts for the final legal approval. In February 2008, we received our final adoption papers and Canadian residency visa. We could finally take our Samantha to Canada, after four years of not being able to leave the Dominican Republic.

"Ask ad it will given to you; seek and you will find; knock and the door will be opened to you. For everyone who asks receives; he who seeks finds; and to him who knocks, the door will be opened."

Luke 11:9

2005 – 2015

Miguel

Meet Miguel. Miguel is your typical young man with a good heart, desire for love, happiness, family and to do something in life. Miguel is the fifth born of six children to his mother. He lives in a poor village in the mountains of the Dominican Republic. His mother does not have work. His Dad has not been a part of his life for most of his life. I do not know how many siblings Miguel has on his father's side. His siblings from his mother do not all have the same father.

Miguel's mother is very typical for mothers in a third world country. She got pregnant as a young teenager from the man who she thought was the love of her life. He was an older man who just wanted a younger girl. She just wanted to be loved, accepted and fill the hole that not having a father in her life had left in her heart. The affections and attention of an older man seemed to help fill in some of the hole in her heart that not having a father had left. Unfortunately, the love story ended, as it does for so many third world young mothers. After a few years, and a couple babies, the man moved on to a younger girl, leaving Miguel's mother on her own with a couple young children.

Over the years, Miguel's mother had a couple more "husbands" and more children. None of the men stayed long. By the time

Miguel was born, his mother was very tired, sad and angry. She is not a Christian and has few friends or family left around her. She is lonely and hurt. And she is tired. She has no energy for raising children anymore. Since Miguel was about two years old, his mother would send him out of the house at daybreak and tell him not to return until it was getting dark. Miguel was on his own to find food, cleanliness, attention and love. He was also on his own to, basically, raise himself.

It truly is amazing how God cares for His children and how resilient the human being is. Miguel is a survivor. God protected Him and Miguel survived. He is alive.

From 2002 to 2005, we had various mission teams come from the USA and Canada to help with our project of changing every house's dirt floor into a concrete floor in the village. When mission teams come down to minister with us, the kids come out and want to hang out with the teams. First, the kids start coming because they see a group of "gringos" and they think that the gringos will give them money, toys, candy, clothes, anything. They also think that it will be easy to take (aka steal) items from the gringos. This is when we first met Miguel.

Miguel was about seven years old when he started to hang out with our teams, and he was difficult. Miguel had never had any real discipline, discipleship or parenting in his life. He did what he wanted, took what he wanted, behaved how he wanted with no thought to others, consequences or right from wrong. He survived. When we first Miguel, we did not know anything about him or his family. As we are there to minister to the people, we do not have a problem with kids hanging out with us and our teams. The first day that Miguel showed up to hang out, he was immediately proving to be a difficult kid. I cannot remember in great detail what Miguel was doing but he was getting into everything and disobeying everyone. He would go through Paul's tool box when no one was looking and try to steal tools. He was a charmer and could charm over the gringos without much effort. Then, as soon as their backs were turned, would try to steal from them. He was always asking for things. For a cookie, a pop, a sandwich, a watch, a pair of shoes, a coat, a camera. He was not shy about asking for anything and everything from team members. Even though there were language barriers, Miguel was able to communicate what he wanted. His constant asking for things was starting to make team members feel uncomfortable.

After a few days of hanging out with the team, Paul felt that he needed to speak to Miguel. He told Miguel that he could not continue to ask team members for things. That he could not ask for anything. Paul told Miguel that he was welcome to hang out with us but he could not ask for anything at all. Miguel agreed and went back to the team. However, his behaviour did not change at all. By the next day, he had asked almost every member of the team for something. Paul and I talked about what we should do in regards to Miguel. We decided that Paul would talk to Miguel again and tell him that if his behaviour did not change, he would be asked to go home and not be allowed to hang with the team. When Paul explained this to Miguel, Miguel seemed to understand and we prayed for some change. Even though we did not know Miguel well yet, we assumed that his home life probably included numerous siblings, a tired mother and no father.

The next day, Miguel continued his begging and asking for things from team members. Paul pulled Miguel aside and told him that he would have to go home and not hang out with the team and why. Paul also told Miguel that he could return the next day. If his behaviour remained unchanged though, then he would have to leave and could not hang out with us. Miguel's behaviour did not change and Paul had to tell him that he could no longer hang out with this team.

A few weeks later, we had another team come from the United States arrive to serve with our ministry and minister to the villagers. Our project of concrete floors continued which put the team and ourselves in the middle of the village, working side by side with the villagers. As had happened with the previous team, kids came out of the wood work to hang out with the team members. We were seeing that what the kids were wanting more than candy or handouts was the love that team members so easily poured out on them. The kids were attention starved and craved to be hugged, given piggy back rides, hold hands while walking down the lane..... to be loved on. Kids are the same all over the world; regardless of country, culture or economic status. They want to be loved and accepted.

Miguel showed up and was hanging back a bit. Paul saw Miguel and went over to talk to him. Miguel asked if he could hang with the team. Paul said that he could but to remember the rules. Paul reminded Miguel that if he broke the rules, he would be sent home for the day and if he broke the rules the following day, he would be sent home for the duration of the team.

Miguel came to the team and started to hang out. He, like the other kids, wanted to be loved; wanted positive attention. You could read the aching on his face. Miguel did a bit better with this team. He did get sent home for the day and then ended up getting sent home for the duration of this team, as well. Between his begging and then his disruptive behaviour as he strove to be the centre of all attention, we just could not allow him to be with the team. Each time, Paul would talk to Miguel, explaining the wrong behaviour and the correct, expected behaviour. Paul would tell Miguel about God, Jesus and tell him that we loved him. Paul would also pray for Miguel each time before sending him home.

As the teams continued to come, Miguel continued to show up. With every team, Miguel would end up getting sent home. With some teams, he would last longer than others, but, he always seemed to mess up and get sent home. Each time, Paul put his arm around Miguel's shoulder, talked with him, prayed with him and shared love. When the next team arrived, Miguel was always there, declaring that he was there to help and that he would make it this time without being sent home. With each new team, we gave Miguel a new chance.

When we did not have a team, Paul would drop by Miguel's house or see Miguel on the dirt streets and hang a bit with him. Paul would ask Miguel about school, home, and how he passed his days. Paul would also share about God, little by little. Paul was building a relationship of trust and care with Miguel; one little step at a time.

As the years went by, Miguel was growing up into a young man. He still came and hung out with our teams all the time. After about two years, a joyous time arrived. Miguel made it an entire team without being sent home!!!! He was improving. Miguel has always had a huge heart to help and an aching heart to be loved. We knew that our job, assigned by God, was to love on Miguel and give him positive directions. Paul's job also included being a positive male influence in his life, teaching him wrong from right. No one had done that before.

At about age 14, Miguel dropped out of school. He did not see a reason to continue. He knew that he would not go to university and any job that he would get would be one that he would be trained to do like working in construction. At age 14, he could get a job as a helper on construction sites, make some money and start to learn a trade. Miguel felt that there was no need to continue with school.

By 2014, Miguel had grown into a young man of 17 years old. He was learning the construction trade and becoming even more helpful with our teams. Over the years, Miguel had become well versed in the rules of our ministry and the do's and don'ts with our teams and for our teams. One of our rules, for team safety, is that when they are walking around the village, they need to always be in groups of two or more. When team members would need to return to the clinic for bathroom breaks or fill water bottles, Miguel would be the first to volunteer to walk with the small groups to ensure that they did not get lost or anything. Miguel has helped to teach teams how to mix concrete, lay blocks and plaster walls.

In the summer of 2014, we had two back to back mission teams from the United States. Miguel showed up with the first team to help and hang out, just like he has been for ten years. On the first team, there were numerous pretty girls who were just a few years older than Miguel. Miguel has always been a charmer and, being a 17 year old teenager, he is no different than any other 17 year old boy in noticing a girl. However, Miguel does not quite know how to behave respectfully around girls as he has had no father to teach him. Miguel was flirting with the girls and there was one girl that he seemed to like more than others. As the team was nearing the end of their time, we learned that Miguel's flirting had grown to a level that it was making one or two of the girls on the team uncomfortable. As soon as Paul learned about this, he pulled Miguel aside to talk with him. They had a long talk and Paul also talked about how God wants a man to treat a woman and how we are supposed to behave and treat others. Once again, Paul presented the Gospel and asked Miguel if he wanted to ask Jesus into his life. Miguel said that he would if Paul wanted him to. Paul told Miguel that it is a personal decision and it has to be real; that Miguel should only pray and ask God into his life if it is real to him and that that is what he wants to do. Miguel said that he did not really want but would pray in order to please Paul. Miguel did not pray that afternoon.

When the second team arrived, Paul gave Miguel another chance but warned him to watch his behaviour and flirting. About four days into the second team, it was shared to us that

Miguel was flirting and made a girl feel really uncomfortable that day when he asked for a kiss. (She did not give him one!). We learned this in the evening. Paul and I talked about what would be the best way to handle Miguel's behaviour. Paul was ready to send Miguel home, as per our ministry rules, however, was hesitant because he knew that Miguel was in a fragile state at this time. We prayed about what to do.

The next morning, Paul and one of our ministry workers, Daniel, pulled Miguel aside first thing to talk to him. They began by going over with Miguel what they had talked about the previous week in regards to Miguel's behaviour and treatment of girls. Miguel was very sheepish and, although listening, not saying much. Paul and Daniel talked with Miguel again about the importance of treating people, especially girls, with respect and kindness. Asking for a kiss was treating a girl with disrespect. They also talked about what God expects from us and why.

Miguel then spoke up and said that God would not want him because of the things that he had done in his life. Things that he has never shared with anyone. Miguel went on to share some of the things that he had done. Things like struggling to not take drugs. Miguel shared how many of his friends use drugs and, even though he had not yet taken any drugs, he struggles with the temptation. He also spoke of other temptations and acts that he had done. Nothing illegal but, for the sake of Miguel's privacy, I am not going to go into detail. The things that Miguel confessed to were things of typical teenage boy actions for a boy not raised with God at the centre. Miguel then confessed to Paul that he really did ache to have God in his heart but is too unworthy. Paul and Daniel both put an arm around Miguel and told him about how God created him, loves him, has plans to prosper him and not to harm him.

Miguel said that he did believe and it was time to ask God into his heart and life. Right there, Miguel prayed. Miguel also asked God's forgiveness for sins committed and God's help to not sin and be a better man. After praying, he asked Paul to translate for him so that he could go apologize to the girl that he asked for a kiss from. They went straight to the team, asked to speak to the girl, Miguel apologized, and forgiveness was given. PRAISE GOD. ALL GLORY TO GOD!

Miguel, as a new believer, has a lot to learn but he has an eager heart and already feels the change of God inside of him. We will continue to counsel, mentor and love him. Please pray for Miguel and that he will walk with our Lord and serve HIM all the days of his life.

Heading out with Medical team to an unreached village for the day. Borrowed another missionary's "tonka" truck so that we could transverse rivers and areas with no roads. May 2008.

Dra. Wendy Diaz thrilled after we received a donation of medications which filled our shelves. The day before, these shelves and cupboards were empty and we did not know what we would do to help our patients.

Typical village house that we replace with a block and concrete house.

Family in front of their new house that our teams & ministry were able to build for them, 2014

Our Staff! Daniel Garcia, Mechy Abreu, Ana Maria Quiroz, Sharyn Branson, Wendy Diaz, Nena Delgado, Paul (Pablo) Branson

<insert Ministry Property here>

La Clinica de Pedregal and Ministry Property. Pedregal de Jarabacoa

Sharyn and Rafelina. Rafelina was 2 when she started to hang around the clinic; dirty, unclothed and seeking love. She is a lovely 13 year old young girl now.

93 students in our School Sponsorship Program, July 2016

Little girl running home after receiving a newly donated dress.

Anny Penalo, our foster daughter, and Sharyn. August 2016

A day of fun with our family: Noah, Samantha, Paul &
Sharyn. August 2016

Paul and Sharyn being interviewed by Missionary Flights
International for their video.

2005

Rachelly

The clinic had been open for about two years and we were seeing new patients on a regular basis, as well as treating our returning patients. One day, the patients were a mother and her six year old daughter, Rachelly. Rachelly stuck very close to her mother, hiding behind her, peeking out at me and not saying a word. I tried to smile at her and make her feel a bit more comfortable. In the Dominican Republic, the cure for most everything seems to be an injection so children are very afraid to go to the doctors.

When I asked the Mom, Rachel, what the main problem was, all that she said was that her daughter could not learn at school. It took a little while of conversing back and forth to get the bigger picture. Rachelly was born hearing impaired, and, as a result, could not speak yet. The family had developed their own type of sign language to communicate so, even though I know sign language, the family did not so I was not able to communicate directly with Rachelly. Rachel tried to put Rachelly in school but Rachelly got teased a lot and she was not able to hear well enough to learn. In the Dominican Republic, outside of the city, there are no schools or programs available to help students who have any type of learning disability, regardless the cause of the disability. Rachel had two other children at home. Her husband drove a truck for a sand company so his income is minimal. The family lives in a village, farther up in the mountain, that at this time, did not have running water or electricity. This is a family without any means to help their daughter.

Rachel explained to me that about six months ago, the entire family (aunts, uncles, grandparents, siblings, cousins) had pulled together enough money for Rachel to be able to take Rachelly to an audiologist (hearing doctor) in the Capital city to get tested. Rachel pulled out some papers from her bag and showed me the results that they had received from the testing. Rachelly's only problem is that she is hearing impaired. The specialist had told Rachel that with the right hearing aids, Rachelly would be able to attend school and lead a normal life. The specialist did tell Rachel that there is no cure for the hearing impairment but there is help out there. The specialist recommended two types of hearing aids. The first choice would cost around $5000 and the second choice would cost about $2000 which is an unimaginable amount of money to this family. It would take about four years of the Dad's complete salary to buy one pair of hearing aids. And that would not include the batteries or regular visits to a specialist for fittings and ensuring that everything is working well for Rachelly. Then, as Rachelly grew, she would need new hearing aids that would fit her growing ears better. What fits her at six would not fit her at 12 years old.

Rachel had heard that we help the poor people and she came to see if we could help her get some hearing aids for her Rachelly. Rachel is a very good mom. She wants the very best for her children. She had travelled on the back of a motor scooter an hour on a dusty, dirt road just to reach our clinic from her home. I told Rachel that I would not make any promises to get hearing aids for Rachelly but that I would use my contacts to see what we could do. I told Rachel that we would all be praying and, if it is God's will to use us, He will provide them. We then prayed together and I told Rachel that we would send word to her if we get any good news. The way to send word to Rachel would be to send a runner to Rachel's brother-in-law who would then send word to a cousin who owns a scooter who would then drive up to Rachel's village to deliver any message. No one had cell phones yet in the mountains or villages. The other way to send a message would be to put it on the local radio station. Four times a day, the radio announced messages from family, friends, etc. for people who live in the villages. It was very effective.

After Rachel left, I shared her need with Ana Maria and we both started to pray for an answer for sweet Rachelly. When Rachelly left, she peaked out behind her mother and gave me a very quick smile. She had already stolen my heart. When I got home that afternoon, I went to my computer and started to send out emails to friends and contacts in the Capital city as well as in Canada and the US, asking if anyone knew of anyway that I could get a pair of hearing aids donated. Hearing aids are very expensive and not something that is easy to find to be donated, especially, to donate to a small, unheard of clinic in the rural mountains of a third world country. Never underestimate God and His connections. A doctor friend of mine knew another doctor who knew another doctor who is an ENT (ears, nose and throat specialist) and he contacted the ENT in Pennsylvania. The situation and need was explained to the ENT. The ENT listened to the story of Rachelly and also looked at the test results and recommendations of the Dominican specialist that I had sent along with my search for help. The ENT told his friend that he agreed with the recommendations of the Dominican specialist and also with the recommendations oforthe type of hearing aid that would be best for Rachelly. The ENT then said that he would donate a set of the hearing aids. He went to his office, and returned with the hearing aids, telling his friend to get them down to me.

When I received the email from my friend telling me this story and that hearing aids were already on their way to me, I was beyond speechless and started to scream my praises to God! I was bouncing off the walls and could not wait to tell Paul and Ana Maria. I decided not to send word to Rachel until we had the hearing aids in our hands. Not that I was doubting God or anything, but I did not want Rachelly to go through the long process of travelling to the clinic and arrive before the hearing aids had arrived. In the meantime, I contacted a Dominican ENT friend of mine who practices in a town about a 25 km away from us, Dr. Baptista. I asked Dr. Baptista if he would be willing to take on Rachelly as his patient as the family did not have the means to return to the Capital city to go to the specialist there. I explained Rachelly's story, and the story of God providing the hearing aids. Dr. Baptista told me to send Rachelly and her mom to him once we had the hearing aids and he would help to fit the aids, for free!

About a week later, the hearing aids arrived. The amount of rejoicing going on, even before Rachel and Rachelly, received word was huge. We sent word to Rachel asking her to come to clinic as soon as possible. It took two days to get word to Rachel and the next day, she showed up at the clinic. She had no idea that we had hearing aids for her Rachelly. When I opened the box with the hearing aids, Rachel's hand went to her mouth and tears started to stream down her face. She was speechless for many minutes. When she did speak, her first words to praise God and then she threw her arms around me. We had about five patients at the clinic at this time, waiting their turn, and everyone was rejoicing and many tears of joy were shed.

I gave the hearing aids to Rachel and the information for Dr. Baptista in La Vega. I told her that Dr. Baptists agreed to do the first consult to fit the hearing aids for free. Two days later, Rachelly and Rachel walked into the clinic. Rachelly had a huge smile on her face and she was looking at everyone and everything. She ran to me and put her arms around me. I looked down at her, saw the hearing aids on her ears and spoke to her. For the first time, she heard me and answered.

Rachel thanked me for sending them to Dr. Baptista and said that they are just on their way home from their first consult with Dr. Baptista. Rachel then proceeded to tell me that Dr. Baptista told them that he will give them one year of free consults and free batteries for the hearing aids for the entire year. What a huge blessing!

Six years later, Rachel walks into the clinic with this lovely, young lady. Rachelly is now twelve years old, almost thirteen. She has been doing well in school, loves to read and study and has taken very good care of her hearing aids. The aids are obviously used, one of the doors to the battery is taped on, but Rachelly is still using them. Rachel asked to speak to me privately in my office. Once in the office, she says that she does not want to ask for more help but that they have tried and tried to get new hearing aids for Rachelly and have not been able to. Rachelly has outgrown the pediatric hearing aids that she received when she was six years old. She needs new ones that fit her now. I said the same thing to Rachel that I told her six years early - if it is God's will, He will provide. When Rachel left, she gave me her cell phone number and asked me to call if anything comes up.

(A lot had changed in the fact that we all now had cell phones but other things had not changed. Rachel and her husband still lived in the same village, there was still no running water to their small house, her husband made about the same amount of money and their needs were great when it came to providing for Rachelly.)

Near our clinic is another ministry's camp and, through their denomination, they host a few American teams each year. As this is a different ministry, we never know what they have going on. About a week after Rachel's recent visit to us, an American walks into our clinic. He explains that he is there with the camp. He tells us that most of the team is doing construction projects on the camp but there is an ENT on the team who brought down her computer, testing programs and equipment to do hearing tests. The camp had not promoted the coming of the ENT so she has all this equipment and fifty sets of hearing aids and no patients. The American was wondering if we have any patients with any kind of hearing needs that we could send to them. The ENT is doing free consults and will give away the hearing aids for free to anyone who really needs them and cannot afford to buy any. I felt the tears come to my eyes. I looked over at Ana Maria and she had a tear or two on her face. God is just so good!

After we composed ourselves, we told this American about Rachel and Rachelly and that just a week early, they came back asking for more help. We also told him that we have about twenty patients in need of hearing tests who cannot afford to go to the city for them and we are pretty sure that at least fifteen of them need hearing aids. Four of these patients were under twenty-five years old. We immediately called Rachel and told her to come right away to the clinic. The next morning, at 8 am, Rachel and Rachelly were waiting for us at the clinic when we showed up. I took Rachelly and Rachel up to the camp to visit the ENT. Rachelly received the first of the fifty pairs of hearing aids that the ENT had brought.

After Rachelly received her new hearing aids that now fit her, she was so happy. She told her Mom that she had to return to my clinic to talk to me. She came to my office and told me how much she thanked God for our clinic and ministry. Rachelly shared with me that most people in her family drink, speak bad and do not go to church but that she knows that there is a God and that He loves her. Rachelly said that she knows this because she has seen how God has used strangers to help her hear and only a real God of love would do this. She told me that she will always keep God first in her heart and life and thanked me for the clinic and sharing about God with her every time that she came to the clinic.

Over the next few days, through getting the word out, many of our patients and friends were able to get their hearing tested. The ENT was able to give away all fifty pairs of hearing aids that she had brought with her.

God has used many, many different people to help Rachelly hear over the years. He has used people in three different countries, different languages and cultures to help Rachelly. Some of the people who have helped Rachelly still has never met her but they were willing to answer God's call for help. We are so thankful to God for all the many ways that He has provided for Rachelly and know that this help will not end.

"For you are a gracious and merciful God."

Nehemiah 9:31b

March 2006

Excerpt from Our Newsletters

MEET MAMATIA

Everyone knows a MamaTia. She is that little old lady in your community, maybe she is even your Grandmother. She is small, petite, has energy and spunk to put us all to shame, loves company, thinks everyone does not eat enough and tells the best stories of the olden days. That is MamaTia. MamaTia is 72 years old, looks older, hauls huge armloads of wood every morning for her fire stove. She has no family, is a spinster, gets paid to look after an man is even older than she is. Mamatia's home, to say it is a falling down shack would be a compliment. We have agreed to improve what she has and build her a home. We had a team here from Saskatchewan in February who were working on MamaTia's home. MamaTia is so grateful that she was buying chips and pop for the team. If they did not eat all that she bought, she was shoving it in their backpacks when they were not looking. All this from an old lady who can not afford to buy her own food. She was a great testimony to us all of the widow who gave one coin in the offering plate with Jesus.

Sharyn Branson

RIGHT PLACE, RIGHT TIME

In June/July, we had a large medical team here and we were working in the southern part of the country amidst a lot of the Haitian sugar cane workers. We were using a school to have our medical clinic in the middle of sugar cane fields. A mother came through the clinic first thing in the morning to have her daughter seen by us. Her daughter was fine, a cold but okay. Three hours after she left us, she returned with her baby girl who had a fever of 103F. This fever developed very fast and the mother was terrified. As we are working in the middle of nowhere, with no lab, we felt our hands tied as we did not know exactly why this baby was so sick so fast. We had suspicions but could not confirm without lab work. The baby was only 22 lbs so we did not want to just guess with treatment. God is so amazing the way that things work out. Our driver was able to take my jeep, run to the nearest town (about 40 mins away), to a lab, run the tests that we needed, get the results and return to us at the clinic site by the time that we were packing up for the day. The tests were positive and, after some mad calculations, two doctors and a pharmacist's double checking the math, we made up the prescriptions and were able to treat this beautiful baby. God is so good in how He pulled everything together to get this baby tested and treated.

September 2006

Excerpt from Our Newsletters

GOD IS WITH US EVEN IN THE BAD

About eight weeks ago I (Sharyn) came to the clinic on a Monday morning to be greeted by word of a terrible incident in the village the night before. A family who lives right in front of the clinic had major problems. The husband (Yunior) had attacked his wife (RoseAna Maria) in front of their two young children and nieces. Yunior beat RoseAna Maria and then came at her with a knife. He cut her arm in two spots and her neck, just missing her carotid artery by 1 cm. The children were not hurt but RoseAna Maria was in the hospital for three days. That night, Paul had bible study in the village and went early to talk with Yunior. Yunior had moved out of the house and to his parents (about six houses away). Neither Yunior nor RoseAna Maria were Christians but RoseAna Maria did have some faith. Paul talked for a while with Yunior then invited him to join the bible study. Yunior has not missed a bible study since that first Monday. I started to talk and counsel with RoseAna Maria once she returned from the hospital. RoseAna Maria's faith has really been increasing at a rapid pace since the attack. She is so open to God and His word and just wants the best for her kids. She wants to follow God and His plan for her family. RoseAna Maria is reading her bible every day, started to attend church and has asked me start up a bible study with her on a weekly basis. I plan to start up a bible study in October. As sad as the beginning of this story is, we are so excited and are praising God for how He used this terrible attack to really draw Yunior and RoseAna Maria closer to Him. RoseAna Maria has accepted Jesus and Yunior is coming along. RoseAna Maria and Yunior started at counselling and are getting along much better. They are still living apart and will continue to until Yunior learns to manage his anger better but there is real hope for this family. Please pray for this family when you think of this story. God is so strong and faithful to us all and just waiting for us to turn to Him. He never leaves us, no matter what!

December 2006

Excerpt from Our Newsletters

GOD WORKS IN MANY WAYS

Paul has been doing a bible study in the village every Monday night for about six months. They have been studying various topics and learning to pray. The people who attend the study are all uneducated, some illiterate but each one loves the Lord. Some are new Christians and some are more mature but they all want to learn more of Him. Paul feels very much outside of his comfort zone doing the bible study but it is what he has felt God has told him to do. As much as he was hesitant to take on the study, he went ahead. The rewards that Paul has received from doing the bible study has been unmeasurable. Sometimes Paul comes home and he does not know who has gotten more out of the study; him or the others who attend. Watching how God is growing the faith of all the people involved in the study has been such an honour.

I believe at one point that I have mentioned a 14 yrs. old girl, Anny, who we are helping to attend the same school as our kids. Anny comes from a very difficult background. She lives in Pedregal with her grandma, aunt and about 22 other family members in a house that is about 20 X 30. Her mother is a prostitute and lives elsewhere in the country. Anny wants to be a doctor one day but with her family background, she has no opportunity. Anny has been working very hard at her school work and English and she is doing fantastic. It is amazing to watch how hard she works and how much she is learning. God has his hand on Anny and is going an amazing work in her. If you think of Anny, say a prayer for her.

"Be strong and courageous.
Do not be terrified; do
not be discouraged for the
Lord your God will be with
you wherever you go."

Joshua 1:9

Spring/Summer 2006

Creation of Sponsorship Program

Education levels vary all over the world. In the Dominican Republic, the government provides free education through the public schools. The Dominican Republic is a country that all school have a uniform, even the public school. The government provides a building for a public school, sometimes pays the teachers and that is about it. The teachers do not have materials, tools or even chalk for the chalkboards. It is no wonder that the education level in the public schools is below standards.

Developing relationships with the local people is essential in order to have the opportunities to share the Word of God. As we were getting to know the people of the village, we were developing relationships. One of those relationships was with a family who lived right across the street from the clinic. The patriots of the family were a grandfather who drank all the time, a grandmother who was tired and raising a bunch of grandchildren. Over time, we learned that two of the daughters lived with their mother as well as five grandchildren. The five grandchildren all have the same mother, but different fathers and were not the children of either of the daughters who did live in the home. The mother of these five children had never lived in the same house as her children. The mother, Analis, is not around and has left her children in the care of her mother, the children's grandmother.

One of these five grandchildren are named Juana. She is the middle child. She started to hang out at the clinic, helping as she could and just wanting to be loved. There was something about Juana that grabbed out attention. She was a smart young girl, currently in grade five in the public school and showing a lot of potential. Like her siblings, she lacked love, attention and parenting in her life. We decided to see if we could help her with her English and then, maybe, she could attend the English mission school in town. Her grandmother agreed and a plan was developed. Juana would take one year off school, work as an assistant to the two year old class at the English school in the mornings and have private English lessons in the afternoons.

After ten months of Juana learning English, she was given the evaluation test by the English school to see if she could enroll as a student. We were all surprised to learn that Juana scored at a kindergarten level in math. Five years in the public school and her math levels were still at a kindergarten level. Juana needed a better education. Juana's English level was now at about a grade 4/5 level. The school accepted Juana and, in September, she began grade five at the English school.

After going through this experience with Juana, our eyes were opened to the level of education that the children were receiving through the public school. God placed it on our hearts to help the children with education. We could not afford to pay the tuition for Juana to attend the English school. God spoke to us to reach out to others to find sponsors to sponsor Juana's education. This is how our school sponsorship program was born with the ministry.

That was in 2005. Today, we now have over 90 students being sponsored in five different private schools who are all obtaining a better education. We have 80 students who have applied for sponsorship and are waiting for a sponsor to select them. We have had twelve students graduate from grade twelve or university. Over 125 have gone through or are currently in our school sponsorship program.

Through the school year, we host various parent and student meetings. At these meetings, we will have a devotion time and also a teaching time. Sometimes, one of the ministry's staff will do the teaching, sometimes we will ask someone else to come. We try to cover topics that are of interest to the students or parents. We have had grade twelve students talk to middle and high school students about the importance of responsibility, studying and getting good grades as a sign of gratitude to their sponsors. This topic was the idea of the students who taught this session. Recently, we did a talk for the parents, and opened it up to the local churches and entire village. The topic that night was about how parents can protect their children on the internet and social media. Internet and social media has reached even remote villages yet the education for the parents has not.

Every day, we are seeing futures being changed and opportunities for the next generation to rise above the poverty and have a better, economic future for themselves and their families.

Here are some stories from a few students from our sponsorship program:

Luisa applied for sponsorship while she was in university studying pharmaceuticals. She was sponsored for her final 18 months of school. Luisa was getting ready to leave school in order to work full time so that she would have funds to complete her schooling. With the sponsorship, she did not have to drop out of university and was able to graduate on schedule. She is now working full time in the career that she trained for.

Jazzie is a smart girl. She has maintained a 90% or higher average her entire life. She the oldest of three kids. Her two younger siblings are both mentally and behaviourally challenged and attend a special need school. Jazzie lives with her mother. Her father left them for another woman shortly after the youngest was born. Jazzie's mother is not educated but she understands that value of a good education. She is faced with the difficulties of raising two special needs children with zero resources. She is a strong woman who loves her children so much. Jazzie works hard at school and hard at home to help her mother. Attending a good school seemed impossible because the only work that Jazzie's mother can get is working for the town cleaning the streets, which does not pay a lot. A couple decided to sponsor this family. Through their love and sponsorship, not only is Jazzie attending a good, private school that has scholarship opportunities for university, but her siblings are now able to attend a special need school. Jazzie is two years away from graduating and still maintains a 90% or higher average in every class.

February - July 2006

Hatillo Land Purchase

We had been living and ministering in the Dominican Republic for nine years. In this time, we had seen God do amazing things. One thing with God; He is never done doing amazing this. One area that we had been praying about was whether to continue to rent housing or to purchase land and build our own house in the Dominican Republic. As foreigners in the DR, it had never been possible to purchase land. The government had a law that said only Dominican citizens could own property in the country. However, about two years earlier, the government changed this law so that now foreigners could purchase land.

We were renting a house that was large enough. We could house mission teams of up to about twelve people in our home and, when we did not have a team, it was a nice family house. Our rent was under what the landlord could have gotten. We had a good relationship with our landlord and he kept the rent very affordable for us.

It was February when our phone rang. Paul picked up the phone and it was a friend of ours from Canada. Our friend, "Joe", explained that he and his brothers had a Christian holding company. He told Paul how for a number of years, the brothers had been lending money to local churches, Bible camps, etc. for various projects (mostly construction repair, renovation or expansion projects). The holding company would set up mortgage style loans and the church or Bible camp would make monthly payments until the loan was paid off. Paul found all this interested but could not figure out why Joe was telling him all this. Then Joe said, "you are wanting to buy land to build your family a house and team housing for mission teams, right?" We had not told people that we were praying, asking God to guide us on whether to try to buy land to build a house and team housing or not. Paul was shocked by Joe's question. Paul told Joe that yes, we have been praying about this but no one really knows that. Joe then told Paul that God had told him and his brothers to contact us and offer a mortgage loan to buy land and build our house. The holding company was interested in building the team housing and having our ministry run it. Joe also said that he felt God telling him to lend us this money so that we could own our house. Then, when the day comes that God sends us back to Canada, we can sell the house and use the equity to buy a house in Canada. What a blessing!

When Paul got off the phone with Joe, he was shocked. He shared the conversation with me and, together, we were shocked. Who receives phone calls like this? God's children do!

Neither of us could really believe this phone call. We did not think that it was real. The way that Joe worded things, Paul was under the impression that the holding company was praying about it and may or may not lend us the money. About five days later, the phone rang. Joe was calling. He asked Paul if he had found land to buy yet? Paul was shocked again as he told Joe that he had not even looked as he still could not believe the offer that the holding company was making us. Joe told Paul that the offer was real and to start looking for land.

The next day, we started to look where some land was available to purchase that was about the size that we were looking for. One of the tricky parts of buying land in countries like the Dominican Republic is that, even though a family may have lived and owned land for generations, they have no legal land title. The family has been on the land longer than the concept of land titles have existed. Or, someone is selling land that is not theirs to sell but they sell it anyways. They take your money and you have no land. You have to be very careful before making any offers to check out the person selling the land (that they have the legal right to sell that land), the family and land titles. Due to all this, it does limit the land that is actually is available to purchase.

We had been looking for about two weeks and still had not found any land that was even a possibility to purchase. A Dominican friend of ours was doing a weekly Bible study in a village about 20 minutes outside of the township. He asked Paul is he wanted to check out some land in this village and offered to go with Paul - as our friend already knew many people in this village. We had never considered this village but we were willing to look. Paul and "Richardo" headed out the next day to the village to see what they could find out. Richardo suggested that they go to the house of one of the oldest families in the village and ask them if they know of any land for sale.

Ricardo and Paul arrived at "Miguel's" house, knocked on his door and waited. When Miguel opened the door, Richardo asked him if he knew of any land for sale in the village. Miguel looked at Richardo, then at Paul and back to Richardo. After quite a pause, Miguel then said that he had some land for sale if they wanted to take a look? The three men headed down a half kilometer trail that ended and opened into a large field where a horse was grazing and was surrounded on three sides by trees and a creek. It was beautiful, off the road with enough land to build a family house and team housing. Miguel, Richardo and Paul walked the land and talked for quite some time.

When Paul came home, he was so excited. He said that I just had to come see the land so, off we went. We drove out to the land and I took a look. I loved it. It was so peaceful..... which in a country with a culture of loud music, loud motorbikes, loud talking - peaceful and quiet is hard to find. In the Dominican culture, land is more valuable right at the road. The farther off the road, the lower in value. This land was half a kilometer from the road. Perfect for us as it was peaceful and lesser price due to, what Dominicans consider, bad location, but what we North Americans think is prime location. Sometimes the differences in cultures are really wonderful!

Paul and I took time to pray while standing on the land to ask God if this was the land HE wanted or not? When we got home, Paul called Joe to tell him about the land. Miguel had given an asking price for the land. It had no amenities. It was just a piece of land. Joe agreed that it sounded good and the price was reasonable as well as within the budget of what the holding company had to loan. It was agreed that we would make an offer and, if accepted, buy the land. The loan would include funds to buy the land as well as build our house. Joe was going to start planning a trip down to see the land, finalize the details of the mortgage with us and sign the purchase papers at the lawyers.

Paul and Richardo returned to Miguel's home to make an offer on the land. Miguel accepted it without negations. The three men then went to the lawyer to draw up a bill of sale. Once the bill of sale was signed, Miguel turned to Paul and said, "I now need to tell you a story." Paul was most puzzled by this statement but sat back, ready to listen to Miguel. Miguel took a deep breath and began.

####"*One night, I had a dream that was so real and vivid that when it was over, I woke up and could not get back to sleep. In my dream there was a man and told me that a gringo was going to knock on my door and ask to buy some land. He told me that I was to sell land to the gringo and which piece of land to sell the gringo. He said to sell it for a fair price because the land would be used for His glory. I woke up, and could not believe the dream. It was so real and vivid yet I had been asleep. The dream bothered me the rest of the night and I never got back to sleep. The next morning, you knocked on my door and asked if I knew of any land for sale. I almost had a heart attack when I saw this gringo at my door, asking to buy land, just like the dream that I had the night before. We looked at the land and you agreed to buy it. All my family and friends said that I was crazy to sell that land to a gringo at the price that I have sold it for. However, they were not in my dream. I know that it was God talking to me. I knew it was real and that it was God as soon as I opened my door and saw a gringo at my door. No gringos live in our village. They never have. You and your family will be the first. This is why I have sold you this land. God told me to and I had to obey God."*

Paul and Richardo sat there, mouths open. They could not believe the story that Miguel just shared, yet, they knew deep in their hearts that Miguel was telling the truth. When Paul came home and shared Miguel's story with me, I got goose bumps all over and knew that God was speaking very clearly! Paul then called Joe and shared the story with him. We all agreed that it was the right piece of land for this project for God.

Buying land is a very long process in the DR. However, once the bill of sale is completed and money exchanges hands, you take possession of the land and wait for the lawyers and government to complete all the land title process. In our case, first the land had to be divided between the Miguel's family. Miguel's Dad owned the land. When he died, the law says that his surviving children equally share the land. However, the family had never legally divided the land. There are ten siblings, two who live out of country. All the siblings agreed to sell the land. The two from out of country flew in and they all signed the necessary documents to divide up their father's land into eleven sections (one for each of them and our piece). This all went quite smoothly. The lawyer guided us as to when to pay the down payments, an installment and then the final payment to the family.

From what we knew, all that was left now was to have the land surveyed and then the lawyer had to file all the paperwork with the land title office, wait on them and then, in about a year, after the file went to the courts to legalize the sale, our title would come out of the land title office. We had hired the only lawyer in the little town, who was also the local magistrate. Other missionaries had used Javier without problem. When we did all this, it was an election year and Javier was running for the congress. What we did not know at the time was the Javier was stealing from his clients to finance his campaign and not doing the legal work that he was hired to do. Paul kept going by Javier's office and with each visit, it was harder to find Javier, talk to Javier or get a straight answer from him or his office.

Meanwhile, on 18 July 2006, we broke land and started to build our house. We hired some friends from the church who are builders while Paul oversaw everything. You always hear so many stories of how horrible it is to build your own house, how it creates marital stress, etc. We are thankful to God that we did not have any of these experiences. It was a lot of hard work, some changes were made as we built, but there was no huge problems, major stress or disagreements. We had a house plan of a main floor with a loft area and the master bedroom upstairs. Due to the slope of the land, we had to build a half basement in order to hold the house up. As this was not in the budget or plans, we just put in the foundation and support columns with plans to build two bedrooms and a bathroom in the future. We did do this, although it took us almost five years to complete that.

On a very rainy, cold, wet December 6, 2006, we moved into our new house. The house was not complete but it was livable. Completed was the main floor (2 bedrooms, open area with kitchen, living room and dining room area and a bathroom).

However, the bathroom was not finished when we moved in. It lacked a toilet. Plumbing was all done but the toilet was not installed. For the first almost 24 hours, the bush was our latrine. Paul installed the toilet the day after we moved in. It was a bit comical and gives us a good laugh up to today. Over the next four months, the loft area and master bedroom were built. First came the stairs to go upstairs. Then, the rest was built, windows installed, etc. For the first couple of months, we lived with no windows upstairs because there were no stairs to get up there. Good thing that we were in the tropics with no below zero temperatures to worry about!

As we continued to minister and work away at the house, the lawyer was supposed to be completing all the paperwork to get the land title completed. After many months, Paul went to Javier's office only to find out that not much had been done. Paul continued to check in with Javier's office, always with the same news. Javier lost the election for congress and it came out that Javier has been using his clients' money to finance his political campaign. Now, Javier had no money and he wanted his clients to pay more in order for him to do the legal paperwork that he had been hired to do. Although not proven in court, Javier had stolen from his clients. One of his clients was a not nice man with criminal activities that included drugs. This man showed up at Javier's home one day to demand his money back. By the grace of God, he did not kill Javier, even though he held a gun to Javier's head. Javier then fled the country and, to our knowledge, has not returned.

A new lawyer came to town. A young lady, fresh out of law school, honest and eager to work with foreigners. Paul went to talk with her to see what we could do. She agreed to take on our case and over the next couple of years, she was able to get our paperwork out of Javier's office. Once Tanya was able to get our paperwork from Javier's office, she was able to look it over. Tanya informed us that Javier had done nothing! He took our money and done nothing. He was supposed to pay the land taxes, which were now two years overdue. Tanya discovered that we had to pay around $4000 in taxes and that nothing else could be done until these taxes were paid. We had already given the money to Javier to pay these taxes so now, we had to pay the money a second time, plus the overdue fines. We sent out a note to ask our friends, families and churches to please join in prayer over all this. In less than two weeks, the $4000 had been donated to pay these taxes (and we had not asked for donations for the taxes, just prayers). God is so amazing!

We were able to get the taxes paid and Tanya was able to proceed to get our land title. After two court appearances, the judge signed off on the sale and legalized all the documentation. Next and final step..... all the paperwork goes to the government's land title office for the official land title to be printed. Tanya informed us that the land title office was about eight months behind in their issuing of land titles. As of May 2014, we are still waiting for our land title to come out of the land title printer's office.

As far as paying for the land, the holding company set us up with a payment program, with 3% interest, and monthly payments of $500. In thirteen years, we will have the land and house paid off. If we return to Canada prior to this, when we sell the property, we pay off the balance of the mortgage and the rest of the sale price is ours in order to buy a house in Canada. God is just so amazing and good in how He uses His children to take care of each other.

Land Purchase

We have been living in the Dominican Republic now for eight years, renting various houses. The house that we were currently living in was too big for us when we first rented it. It is two stories on half an acre with four bedrooms and two and a half bathrooms. For just the two of us, it was huge. However, over the six years that we have been renting it, we have housed many teams, had many guests, and grew our family with two beautiful children.

When we first looked at the house, it was too big and the landlord was asking a price that was out of reach for our budget. The house had been vacant for a year and the landlord wanted to get the house rented. The landlord made us an offer that we could rent it for what we could afford (which was half of what he was asking) and that they would not raise the rent for two years if we rented it as is. We agreed. God is good. Over the course of six years, the landlord raised our rent only twice. When we moved out of this house, our rent was $5500RD. The next tenants into the house paid $13,500RD. God, as always, was so good to us in keeping the rent at what we could afford yet providing us with a house that more than met our needs.

"Has not God chosen those who are poor in the eyes of the world to be rich in faith and to inherit the kingdom he promised those who love him."

James 2:5

Racism

This will be a touchy chapter and it will probably make a bit uncomfortable. However, I do not believe that feeling uncomfortable is not necessarily a bad thing. We can never grow and stretch out of our comfort box if we are always comfortable. In today's day and age, in the first world, most people do not know what true discrimination is. The word "discrimination" is used a lot but many who use it in the first world have never truly been discriminated against. Some have, do not misunderstand me, and to those who have, I am truly sorry that this has happened to you. Being discriminated against affects you for the rest of your life.

The island of Hispaniola has a long history. The first people of the island were Indians called "Taine". No one knows much about this people group because when the Spaniards came to the island, they eventually killed all the Taine Indians. The only evidence of the Tainos is art found on the walls of caves around the island. After Christopher Columbus discovered the island of Hispaniola, the French came and it also became a major stop over on the African slave trade route. The people of the island of Hispaniola come mainly from descendants of Spain, France and Africa. Hundreds of years ago, there were wars between the French and Spanish to gain control of the island. In the final war, Spain won. They chose the eastern side of the island as it was closer to Spain, which is today known as the Dominican Republic. French got the west side; which today is known as Haiti. Racism is as old as man and many have believed that the whiter skin that you have, the more superior that you are. Due to this belief, the Spanish sent the Africans to the western side of the island with the French.

In Haiti's early history, the French were the elite and ruled the country, while the Africans served the white man. There was a huge span in every aspect of the culture from economics to attitudes between the rich French and poor Africans in Haiti. This trend has not changed much over the generations. In the Dominican Republic, as there was more Spanish blood than African blood in their history, their skin colour, on average, is a lighter brown. Whereas, Haitians usually are quite dark, like their African brothers and sisters. The attitude of "lighter skin is more superior" is an attitude that is very real today in the Dominican Republic. For example: if two people apply for a job, the lighter skin person will usually get the job; even if the darker skinned person is more qualified. You see this attitude reflected in level of society and it does not end. This attitude is strong throughout the entire Dominican culture, regardless of economic or educational status.

We had heard about the dislike between Haitian and Dominicans but before having our own children, we had not ever been in the middle of any of this. We heard that there was discrimination against the Haitians but had never really seen it. It was just something that you hear about. Then, on Christmas Eve 2001, we brought home our son from Haiti, where we adopted him from. A few days after bringing our son home, we put him in the stroller and headed out for an afternoon walk. As we were closing the gate to our property, a neighbour was walking by. She stopped and asked us if we had a baby? We answered that yes, we had just adopted a son. She bent over to take a look at our new son and her smile quickly went away. She looked up at us and said "How could you bring that thing into my country?" and she walked away. Paul and I both stood there speechless. We looked at each other, confirmed that we had both heard the same words and felt so sad, angry and hurt. As Spanish is our second language, we were both hoping that we had misunderstood. However, we had not, she had really said those horrible words. How can anyone hate an innocent baby? That was our first experience with true racism and discrimination.

Unfortunately, we started to hear, and have to learn to ignore, name calling. We would walk down the street with our son and hear people say call our son racist names. Literal translation means ugly little black thing and charcoal but in the Dominican and Haitian cultures, these words are as significant, racist, hurtful and potent as the "n" word is in English.

One day, I was at the cargo side of the airport as it was mail day for us. (Our mail is brought into the country and taken out of country twice a week by a mail ministry called Missionary Flights Organization (MFI). When MFI flies into the country, we meet the plane at the airport to collect our mail.) I was waiting for MFI to land and had my son, Noah, with me. Noah was only about three years old and we were just walking around the hanger as we waited for the mail plane to land. There was security guard standing near us, doing his job at the hangers. As Noah and I walked by, Noah was about five feet in front of me and the security guard called Noah a racist name as Noah passes him. Every once in a while, you say the right words at the right time. I believe that this was a prompting by the Holy Spirit and God's words that left my lips. I stopped and asked the guard if he had any children. Dominicans, like most people, are very proud of their children. If you ask about their family, you are giving them a huge compliment. The guard put on a smile, said, "Yes, I have two children" and he proceeded to pull out his wallet to show me pictures of his children. They were very attractive and cute children; of which I said so to the guard. I complimented him on his children, asked their names and ages. He was very happy to tell me about his beautiful children. I then pointed to Noah and said, "That is my son. How would you like it if I was to call your children the same name that you just called my son?" The guard was speechless. About fifteen minutes, he approached me and apologized to me for calling my son a terrible name. I was impressed that this man came up to me fifteen minutes later to apologize. He could have just let it go, but he did not. I prayed that our conversation would make a mark on this man's life and that he would never look at a dark skinned person like that again. Also, that he would teach his children not to discriminate based on the colour of one's skin.

We started Noah in preschool at an American started missions school that had mostly Dominican children and few foreign missionary kids. This was not a good experience. Noah stayed at the school for a few years, and when Samantha, our daughter, came of age, she, too attended this school. Unfortunately, kids do repeat what they hear and learn at home. Our kids were, once again, discriminated against because they are Haitian and darker skinned. One American teacher would watch Noah at lunch and said that it was like Noah orbited the playground - he did not interact with other kids and other kids did not interact with him. If something went wrong in the classroom, our kids were always blamed for it. Most times, it was not our kids' fault. Every day, we received phone calls from the school with a bad report. One night, just before Christmas, after we had tucked the kids into bed, I heard Noah start to pray. I stood outside of his doorway to listen. I started to cry as I heard my dear son pray "Dear God, please change my skin colour so that I can have a friend?" The next day, we withdrew our children from school and began the world of home schooling.

This chapter can very much read as being very negative towards Dominicans. The Dominican culture, due to their history between the two countries, is the biggest culprit of this racist attitude. It is fueled some in today's society but it is very ingrained into the culture and passed down from generation to generation to generation. Some of our very best friends in the whole world are Dominican. We continue to minister to Dominicans, in the Dominican Republic. Not all Dominicans think and believe like the attitude that we have experienced. There are very good people in the Dominican Republic who are not racist at all. In fact, they work hard to help the Haitians who live in their communities and express their kindness.

June 2007

Water System

One of the major problems with heath care in a third world country is clean water. Not only is access to clean water difficult, but a greater difficulty is changing the way that people who live in a third world believe that it does not matter. They have lived for generations with unclean water. They believe that "this is normal" as they have never known any different in their entire lives. Bad water and water that makes you sick is the norm - this is what the locals have always had. They believe that parasites are normal and unpreventable. They do not believe that water can make you sick as it is a necessity of life so why would it be making you ill. This generational train of thought is the biggest hurdle you have when you enter a village, and wanting to bring them clean water. First, you have to teach them and pray that they will believe that they need clean water and to stop using the unclean water that they have used their entire life. If the water looks clear, then how could be making them ill? The local people have spent their entire lives with limited sources of water. "Yes, water have made them ill and caused parasite but everyone has this same problem so it is okay and it is normal." This is what the people believe, mostly because they know no different. We wanted to show them what clean water is and that their new normal could include not contracting parasites and illness from the dirty water.

In 2003, the YWAM ministry approached us to partner with them on a project. YWAM had a team coming to the country from the USA called "Living Water". Living Water brings entire water purification systems, work with the local people to train a group of local men to clean and maintain the system and then also train some ladies to teach health education in regards to clean water. We loved the idea of partnering with YWAM on the water project. It has always been a goal to help the villagers to improve their health and educate them in ways that they can prevent diseases.

In order to bring this water system into the village, we needed to have the cooperation of the village and the desire of the village to want the system. In the DR, like in many cultures, each village has its own "mayor" and "council". In the DR, it is called "La Junta de Vecincos". Without the approval and support of the Junta, we knew that it would be pointless to try to install a water purification system into the village. Paul found out when the next meeting of the Junta would be and asked if he could attend and address the council. They agreed and invited him to come. Paul went and presented the idea of bringing in a water treatment system for the village. He explained that the village would have to donate the land, build the small building to house the treatment system, get ten men to volunteer to help install the system and be trained on maintaining and repairing the system. Paul also explained that we would need ten ladies to volunteer to work with me to take some training on clean water and then they would go door to door to every house in the village to teach family the importance of drinking and using only clean water. The Junta agreed that they would like the water system and would work with us to obtain it.

The next step was for Paul to work together with the Junta to get a small piece of land donated and then build the small building that will house the water system. The village had one month to complete this project. A family in the village donated a small piece of land that is about 10' x 15'. It is not very large but is plenty enough large to build the size of building needed to house the water treatment system. The land is located on the main road, at the entrance to the village so very central for everyone. We are all very thankful to this family. Then, various families donated a little bit of money until the village had enough money to buy the bricks, cement and sand to build the small building and work began. It did not take the men very long to build the building and it was completed before the team from Living Waters arrived in our village.

The day came that the Living Waters team was to arrive in our village. Paul, myself and the Junta were all on hand to receive the group. They arrived and were pleased with the building that the men of the village built to house the water purification system. Ten men from the village had been selected who would work with the Living Waters team as they installed the system. Paul and these same men would learn all about how the system works, how to take it all apart, how to clean and maintain it, how to troubleshoot and repair the system when a problem occurs. As they these ten men worked side by side with the Living Waters team, they learned all about the system and were trained to be able to maintain the system long after the Living Water team left the country.

While the men were building and installing the water purification system. A couple ladies from the Living Water team and myself started to meet with ten women of the village who had volunteered. We spent three days teaching and training these ladies all about contaminated and purified water. Included in this training was teaching the difference between contaminated and pure water, why pure water is necessary, why go to the effort to get pure water when there is clear water coming from your tap (even though it is contaminated), etc. Then, we spent time training these ten ladies how to teach about pure water and why it is important to use only pure water and not use contaminated water.

At about the same time that we were finishing training the ladies, the men were finishing installing the purification system. The men were testing the system and having great success. The Junta and the men were very excited about the purification system. It was all working well. The men were feeling confident in their knowledge of the system and ability to maintain and repair it. The ladies were educated and ready to go out. A 5 gallon of pure was selling for $25RD. The Junta decided that they would sell 5 gallons of pure water for $10RD (about 25 cents).

The ladies began to go out in groups of two, going door to door to every house in the village. Their goal was to teach every household about the difference between contaminated and pure water and why it is so important to drink and use only pure water. With the new water purification system right there in their village, the villagers no longer needed to go into the nearest town to get water. It was now easy, quick and accessible to bring pure water into their homes. It was a big job to educate every household, however, it was important and had some success. The ladies were very dedicated and they taught every household in the village.

It has been thirteen years since we installed the water purification system. The Junta still operates the system. Pure water is available for purchase to all the villagers, and for anyone else who comes to purchase it. It is still sold at 65% less than in the grocery stores. The men of the village still maintain and repair the system and it is also provided full time employment for one man who runs the system and sells the water. To this day, the water purification system is still in full operation, providing pure water for whomever would like it.

"In the last times there will be scoffers who will follow their own ungodly desires. These are the men who divide you, who follow mere natural instincts and do not have the Spirit."

Jude verse 18-19

2007

The Witch Doctor

In the Bible, we read in the history about great spiritual battles that took place between God and satan, between man and satan and his demons. Sometimes, we can forget that these spiritual battles have not ended just because 2000 or 5000 years have passed. God is God; He never changes. As a result, satan keeps trying to attack and foil God's work and His children who do His work.

We have personally experienced and witnessed many spiritual battles as the enemy attacks and tries to stop God's works. In the village that we have ministered in for many years, we have seen the enemy attack. When we started to minister in Pedregal, there was a Pentecostal and an Episcopal church. There was no voodoo or witch doctor; of which we were thankful for. Not that the enemy never attacks, however, there was no one person being used by him to attack.

One day, things instantly changed. We heard that a witch doctor had moved into the village. He had set up his flag pole with his black flag. When the flag is raised, it means that he is in and available. When it is lowered, it means that he is not available. In his back yard, he constructed three crosses which he put in the ground at the end of the yard.

Before the witch doctor moved into the village, we were versed in spiritual warfare, had our own experiences with the battles and knew a bit about voodoo. Now, we had to start learning a lot more in order to be prepared to fight the battles ahead. One of the first thing that we wanted to learn was the significance of the three crosses. We are familiar with the three crosses at Calvary when Jesus was crucified but why would a witch doctor have three crosses in his yard? What we learned was that the crosses are for people to lay their petitions and offerings to the witch doctor. The cross on the right is for petitions of gain or want. Financial gain, good health, getting someone out of jail, wanting something. The cross on the left is for petitions asking for curses to be laid on someone. The middle cross is for petition of death where you would ask for someone to die.

A person will go to the cross that matches their petition, lay down their request and financial offering and leave it to the witch doctor to work his voodoo to accomplish this. We also learned that one way that witch doctors will accomplish the petitions is through bribery and corruption. For example - if your son was arrested, you would lay your petition and money at the cross, then, the witch doctor takes a portion of the money to bribe the police into releasing your son and pockets the rest of the money for himself. You believe the voodoo freed your son, not knowing that the witch doctor bribed the police with some of the money that you paid him.

In the first four weeks after the witch doctor moved into village, four people died and two were permanently injured in accidents. One of the deaths occurred when a young man of 22 who never drank alcohol, for some unknown reason, spent an afternoon at the local bar, drank so much that he was intoxicated beyond control, got on a bicycle and rode it into a brick wall. His head hit the wall and he died instantly.

Another person, who had no medical history of seizures, one day had a gran mal seizure and died within fifteen minutes. No history of seizures and no one his family has any history of seizures. A youth, who never rode a motor scooter before, was too young to ride one, and had never shown any desire to ride one, stole a scooter, rode it and drove right into the front of a car - dying at the hospital within an hour of the accident.

The deaths that took place after the witch doctor came to the village are still, to this day, unexplainable. The behaviour that the people who died displayed on the day of their death was completely and 100% out of character for these people. The only explanation that we can provide is that it was the enemy and he was working hard to plant his roots into our village.

The Body of Christ came together very quickly and we all started to pray, fast and spiritually fight spiritually the attacks of the enemy and against the witch doctor. The witch doctor had the legal right to live in this village so we knew that they only way to win against him was with the power of God. God is more powerful than satan. Have you read God's book? He wins!

The witch doctor has since left our village and we praise God that HE won!

August 2007

Excerpt from Our Newsletter

THE ANGELS REJOICE

In our ministry, sometimes seeing those glorious results are slow coming. We sow a lot of seeds but we are not always the ones who see the seed grow and break through the soil. The other night was one of those times that God allowed us to be part of the ground breaking. Paul was having his weekly bible study in the Pedregal and the mother of the host was visiting from her village. We have known Maria for a few years. She is elderly, the mother of four kids. This night, she made the decision to ask Jesus into her heart and to follow Jesus the rest of her life. WOW. How very exciting. Paul was able to lead Maria in prayer and the whole group rejoiced afterwards. God is so amazing!!!

We had three construction teams since our last newsletter so work has really progressed on the two houses that we are building. Our first priority is Altagracia's house. She lives between her Mom and sister. All three houses are in terrible shape. The worst are Altagracias's and her Mom's. As we can not do three houses at once and leave them all homeless, we all agreed to start with Altagracia's. When her house is complete, her mom will move in with her while we rebuild mom's house. The houses these families are living in are falling down and every time that it rains, they literally have about six to ten inches of water running through their house. Altagracia's house became so bad that she had to flee her house and rent a room from her sister for herself and kids.

The walls, roof, base of the floor and plastering are done. Now we have the electrical, plumbing, doors, windows and couple other details and then the house is done. We pray to get it done in the next month or so, money allowing.

We are now booking teams for next year. If you or your church are thinking of getting involved in missions - a mission trip is a great opportunity. Contact us for more information.

March 2008

Excerpt from Our Newsletters

YOUTHS......

Whenever we have a mission team with young ladies from another, the local male youth love to hang out with the team. Our last team was no exception. Usually, it is such a struggle because the local youth can be a real bother in many ways to the youth on team. However, with our last mission team, this was not the case. Yes, the male youth still came to hang around but they were not the usual bother. This time, they were more earnestly curious as to why these peers from another country would come all the way here to help them? Some very interesting conversation took place between the youths and seeds were planted. Now, these local youths are asking if they can come to church with us. Due to the youth's genuine interest in our Lord, Paul is going to start up a social group/ bible study with these youths and see where it takes us all.

TEAMS

January and February brought us three teams that kept us busy. The first was a father and son team who came for about a week to make and distribute reading glasses for the local people. They also trained up one local person to make and sell the reading glasses and left her with a nice stash of supplies.

Later in January, we had a great, first time team, from North Carolina. Most on this team had never done anything like this and it was a great success. This church is now planning to send down two teams a year. Then we had our annual team from northern Saskatchewan. It was great to see some new faces and renew friendships with others who were returning. With both of these teams, construction projects were completed, friendships were made, the word and love of God was shared and people came closer to Jesus and God our Father. All these teams were such a huge blessing in so many, many ways!

"In the same way, I tell you, there is rejoicing in the presence of the angels of God over one sinner who repents."

Luke 15:10

2008

Dra. Wendy Diaz

The clinic had been operational for 7 years and growing all the time. The patient load was increasing to the point that the clinic could be open full time, however, I did not have the time, nor did the doctors who came once or a twice a week. We found ourselves in the position of the "good" problem of maybe needing to find a full time doctor for the clinic. I had not given this too much thought at all. The thought of maybe looking for a full time doctor had crossed my mind just once or twice. Then one day, Ana Maria, handed me a piece of paper with a name and phone number scribbled on it. She said that this person wanted to talk to me and I should call her. I asked who this person was and she said a pastor and someone who works in medicine who wanted to talk to me. This person had never met me before.

A couple days passed, and Ana Maria asked if I had called yet. I said no and that I had forgotten. Finally, after a couple more days, I called, asked for a Wendy Diaz and introduced myself. Wendy said that she needed to meet me with if I would be kind enough to have the time. We made arrangements to meet at a coffee shop in town, in the middle of the afternoon, the following Saturday. When I showed up, Wendy was waiting with a man, whom she introduced as her husband. I introduced myself and we all sat down. I asked Wendy what she wanted to talk to me about. She proceeded to tell me that her and husband pastor a church, that they have three boys and that she is a doctor who works at a clinic run by the government. Wendy told me that although she had been working at this clinic for almost five years, she did not get much joy out of it and she was not able to share about God with the patients as she really wanted to. She said that she had heard about me and my clinic and she would like to learn more about. I proceeded to tell Wendy a bit about myself, my family and the clinic. Then, without making any commitments, I invited to come out one day and see the clinic. Wendy said that she and her husband would talk about it and let me know.

A few days later, Wendy and her husband arrived at the clinic to see it. We spent about an hour together talking about the clinic and Wendy's medical background. Wendy told me that, if I wanted, she would be willing to quit her clinic job and come work for our ministry. We talked a little about pay, work hours, etc. The typical stuff. After prayer and conversation, we hired Wendy. She started at half time, working when I was not so that the clinic could be open full time. As my responsibilities started to change, Wendy took on more hours until she became the clinic's full time doctor. Today, she is charge of the medical clinic and supervises all visiting doctors and specialists.

A few years later, Wendy shared with me how she came to hear about me and the clinic. Wendy had a very vivid dream one night. A dream so vivid that she woke up and remembered every aspect of the dream. In the dream, she felt God talking to her and that He said to "find Sharyn Branson and work at her clinic". Wendy was confused by this as she did not know any foreigners and had never heard of me. She recognized that the name was not Dominican and assumed that I was a foreigner. For the first day or so, Wendy kept this dream to herself but the feeling that she had to find out who this Sharyn Branson is never went away…... it just increased. She started to ask around a bit with some of the other doctors in town if they knew a Sharyn Branson who had a clinic in the area. Wendy asked two doctors and they both knew me. They told them about me and my clinic and how to get a hold of me. Wendy knew from the moment that she woke from that dream that she would be changing jobs to work for me but had no idea why.

Over the years, God has used Wendy in so many amazing ways. She has grown her own patient load, she prays with every patient, some people come to the clinic just for counsel and prayer from Wendy. Now, Wendy has gone back to university, attending one day a week and studying throughout the week, to become a certified family therapist. Through her practice at the clinic, she (as well myself) see a huge need for family therapy and Wendy felt God saying that she is the one to get this training. Wendy is a blessing to every one of our patients as well as the ministry and myself!!

November 2008

Excerpt from Our Newsletters

THREE STORIES.......

Elva is a sweet lady, older and a recent widow. Her husband was killed in a motorbike accident in April when he was returning home and young man who was drunk hit him head on. Delgado's death was a shock to us all but no one more than his wife of almost forty years. Delgado was hoping to replace the roof on his house this summer as the tin was over fifty years and leaked horribly whenever it rained. Elva is a strong Christian and put all her faith in our Heavenly Father. In October, through a team from North Caroline, we replaced Elva's roof and she is now sleeping in her bed, without leaks, whenever it rains.

Three Sunday ago, at a church service of a church plant in town, there were a large number of youths who, for some reason only God knows, decided to attend the service that afternoon. When the preacher asked if anyone was there who wanted to ask Jesus into their heart, fifty (50) of these youths went forward, dropped to their knees and asked Jesus into their hearts and to change their lives. God is so amazing.

Another day, a young woman was pregnant, unmarried and going into labour. Her fiancé, who was not the birth father, was frantically trying to find her help. He could not find her any help at all and was getting so desperate. He was praying so hard for God to help and God does not leave us, especially in our time of need. He provided help and a place for this new mom to deliver her baby son.

What do these three stories have in common. First off, they are all true. Second, God was working, providing and changing lives in special ways. Third, God was using others to help His children in need. Fourth, God is always there for you. The first two stories happened in the past couple months. The third story happened 2008 years ago. However, time means nothing to God as He does not change and does not leave us. As the world comes together in the name of peace to celebrate Jesus' birth, let's remember our neighbours, friends and family and help them as we can. Let's also remember to put the honour, glory and focus where it belongs..... on Jesus, on God. He is our Father!

2008

Present Day

Dick & Henry - Best Friends Forever

In 2008, we were hosting and working with a medical team while serving with Medical Ministry International (MMI). MMI brings in medical teams for a 14 day period. For the medical teams, we take them to different villages each day, for ten days, to do one day medical clinics in remote villages and areas. As we never know how many patients will come each day, some days are super busy and some days a bit slower. It is during these slower times that we are blessed to be able to get to know the people who have sacrificed to come down to the DR to serve for two weeks.

It was during the slower times that both Paul and I were able to start to get to know two gentlemen who were on the team. They were a tad older than most of the people on the team and had come together. Dick was a retired high school teacher and was helping with showing patients where to go from station to station. Henry is an EMT with his local fire department. Henry was working at the check in area, taking blood pressures and weights for each patient who came in.

One of our funniest Henry stories came during one of the slower days that we were having in a remote village. It was hot, slow and Henry had dozed off for a quick snooze. An older lady came to see the doctors. She registered at the front then was directed to come visit Henry. When the lady approached Henry, she hesitated, bent over and took a good look at Henry. Then she turned to Paul and ask, "Is he dead?" We all could not hold back our laughter, which woke up Henry.

Henry and Dick enjoyed the area that we are located and, after returning home, asked if they could return to serve with our ministry. The following year, Dick and Henry came down at the same time as a team from Charlotte, NC. You would never know that they had never met anyone on the team prior to coming down. They fit right in.

In the years to follow, Dick and Henry return to serve with our ministry for two weeks every year. They always come the same time as another team, however, sometimes the team is coming for only a week so Dick and Henry will come for a few days before the team and leave a few days after team. They have blessed us and our ministry so very much over the years. They encourage us, they help so many people, they encourage, and the lead by example.

Dick and Henry have been friends since kindergarten and have remained the best of friends. They are a real inspiration to us. They are both married to the same ladies that they married when they were much younger; both of them having been married for over 50 years each. Their entire lives are a living testimony to Christ and an example for all us to learn from. It is a real honour to call these two amazing gentlemen our friends and to look up to them in a fatherly way.

Paul and Dick have spent many, many hours in great theological conversations as the banter back and forth. It is fun to listen to them. Henry and Paul share a love of wood working and can spend hours in a shop together. Their example of serving God and putting God first in every area of life has been a lesson and example to us.

Paul, Dick and Henry can banter back and forth for hours. Our favourite photos of these three is of them in the "hear no evil, see no evil, speak no evil" pose with each one of them depicting on those. The photo really does show exactly how much fun we have together and how much these three men love each other.

March 2009

Excerpt from Our Newsletters

GOD IS MOVING

Since January, we have been honoured to be part of six people's lives who have asked Jesus into their lives. Here are a couple of their stories. Paul has been doing a Monday bible study for year and in January, he started a Wednesday bible study with a new family to Pedregal. The very first night that Paul had a bible study, the entire family (wife, husband and wife's father) asked Jesus to enter their lives. Ever since that night in January, the bible study has continued and the faith in this household is growing stronger every day.

Giovanny is the driver that we hire to transport our teams. For years, Paul has been witnessing to Giovanny. Giovanny always thought that he had to change everything in his life in order to accept Jesus. He thought that he could not work because in his type of work as a hired driver, he works many Sundays. This always prevented him from asking Jesus into his heart. In February, when Giovanny and Paul were on a three hour drive to Puerto Plata to pick up a team, Giovanny asked Jesus into his heart. Paul said that Giovanny was so emotional that he almost drove right off the road. Giovanny is also growing stronger in his relationship with Jesus every day.

"I am with you and will rescue you, declares the Lord." Jeremiah 1:8

May 2009

Flood that Separated our Mission Team

It is the middle of May, which, in the mountains of the Dominican Republic, is one of the rainy seasons. It is very typical for the rains to start mid afternoon and continue until the early hours of the morning. The sun will come out for a few hours and then it will rain again. It can go on like this for the entire month of May.

In May 2008, we were very busy as we hosted a medical team through *Medical Missions International.* This was a team of about 45 people. The team was split into two groups. One group was the surgical team. They would travel from the camp to a private Christian clinic that we often partner with and do surgeries for people in need, who otherwise would not have the means to obtain the surgery that needed. The other part of the team was the clinical team. We would all load up on the yellow bus and head out to a different village every day for ten working days. While in the village, we would set up for the day in a church, school, maybe some houses, under mango trees, etc. and provide medical consultations, basic lab work, medications and health educations to whomever came to see us from that village and surrounding areas.

One afternoon, both teams ended up finishing for the day early and being back at the camp at around the same time. As we had about 90 minutes before dinner/supper time, and some of the team had yet to have a break to go into the town to look around, pick up some snack food, buy an ice cream, etc., we decided to take those who wanted to go into town for a short trip. Town is only about a ten minute drive from the town. The plan was to go to town, spend about 45 minutes there and be back in plenty of time for dinner. Not everyone on the team wanted to go to town, and that was okay. Those who wanted to go, jumped on the bus, and off we went. Paul took the group to town while I headed home with our kids in our vehicle. Just before we all left the camp, it started to rain heavily. We were okay with this as we were driving to town so off we went. About 30 of the team jumped on the bus.

It continued to rain while the group was in town and it rained! It was tropical, torrential rains. It is quite something to experience precipitation of such magnitude. It is like a faucet has been suddenly turned on super high. The skies opened up and all the water falls. The rain falls so fast and so hard that if you are driving, you literally cannot see the end of your vehicle. It is like a white out snow storm only with rain. Gutter and ditches will flood in minutes. River levels will rise right before your eyes. And then, just as suddenly as the torrential rains started, they stop. The faucet gets instantly turned off. However, the water left behind will take longer to dry up than an instant. This is the rain that started as we headed into town with the group.

To get to town from the camp, we have to drive over a short bridge that is about 150 metres long and goes over the Rio Baguate (Baguate River). The bridge is about 30 feet above the usual level of the river. We have lived here since 1997 and the biggest problem that we have with the river when it rains is how muddy and dirty it becomes.

About an hour after leaving the camp, the team is returning to the camp. The bridge is about three quarters of a kilometre from the camp. When the bus approaches the bridge, the road is blocked by cars, trucks, motorbikes and people. The bus stops while Paul gets out to see what is happened. In the ten minutes that it rained, the river flooded and washed away the bridge! A quarter of the bridge plus two houses had been washed away. Thankfully, no one was injured or carried away into the river - Praise God!

The river below is rushing fast and it is way too dangerous to try to go into the river and cross. We have a problem. A quarter of the team, plus the cooks, food and the team's clothing, personal items and accommodations are on the other side of the camp. Our co-leader is on the other side, too. We have the bus on our side plus 3/4 of the team. So - they have the food, clothing and beds while we have the transportation. And who knows when the bridge will be fixed?

It is getting late, stores are all closed, people are hungry and some are a little anxious. We need to do something. Paul calls me to tell me about the situation. I suggest to bring the team to our house while we figure things out. About 40 minutes later, I hear a group of voices as the team has been dropped at the main road and walked the .4 km to our house from the road. (Our entrance is too small and narrow for the bus to fit in so it has to park on the main road.) As the team reaches the house, it is obvious that they are tired, hungry and little uncertain as to what will happen next. \

People come into the house and start to find places to sit or roam. I head to the kitchen to see what I can find. I had fed my kids earlier, before Paul had even called. Now I had about 40 people in my house who needed food and, as the culture is, the grocery stores in town are closed, plus, we did not have much money on us as we only take what we need with us when we leave the camp. A couple of the ladies from the team joined me in the kitchen and we started looking to see what I had. We made up a dinner that was like nothing that the team had eaten yet. We basically cooked up what we found. A bit of leftovers. A pot of rice. Spaghetti and sauce. Salad. Fruit. Pancakes. French toast. Potatoes. Juice. Water. Coffee. It was an interesting meal and interesting combination of foods but everyone got enough food to be full and content and that was all that matter. God had provided for our unexpected 40 dinner guests.

While I cooked, Paul was on the phone to various friends trying to figure out where everyone would sleep. They could sleep at our house, literally taking over every bit of floor space, but that would be without bedding as I did not have bedding for 40 people. We were limited to what was available on our side of the bridge. A friend of ours runs a tourist resort with cabins that is only about 1.2 km from our house. When Paul called Angel and told him our situation, he said that he had no guests for the night so the entire place was available and could accommodate our team. Angel was not even going to charge us as he wanted to help out in this emergency. Praise God!!! We also were able to use this opportunity to evangelize to Angel, who is a rough ex US marine.

The next day became a day of problem solving. Angel had food at his resort and generously, together with his wife, cooked a great breakfast of eggs, bread and coffee for the team. While the team relaxed on both sides of the river, Paul, our co-leader, Dan and myself worked on ways to get the team together on our side of the river, new accommodation and get the team to the hospital and village that they were suppose to be ministering at on this day. As you can imagine, it was a late start to the day for the team as they had to sit around and wait for us to get things figured out.

By 10 am, we had a new camp to house the team at on this side of the river. The ones that were with us were able to go to the hospital to serve our patients. We found a way to cross the river so that people could get their necessities - whatever they could carry. Our way across was by obtaining permission from the owner of private property who had a walking bridge that crossed the river. He allowed us onto his property and to use his bridge. The bridge came out on the other side just a few "blocks" from the camp where the rest of the team was. It was great to walk into the camp and reunite the team. Everyone collected their personal items, packed up the rest of their stuff and, with the entire team together, we hiked back across the river to the bus.

The ministry owns a large panel truck that is used to move medical equipment, kitchen, and suitcases from location to location. This truck was at the camp so our staff loaded everything up and took off for a long drive. There is a road on the other side of the river, where the camp is, that goes up over the mountain, back down and comes out on the main highway. Then you can take the highway to our mountain road and come back to town, on the other side of the river. It took our driver about 5 hours to make this trip but later that night, he rolled into the new camp where dinner was waiting and a team of happy people who could now have their suitcases.

It was a very long 30 hours but everyone, and all of their possession, were together again on the same side of the river. We praise God that no one was hurt.

In true Dominican ingenuity, the Dominicans rigged up a way to walk across the bridge before the first day as out. They rigged up a way to drive across it in a few days. About ten months later, the bridge was properly repaired and, as of this writing, has not washed away.

November 2009

Excerpt from Our Newsletters

USING ALL OPPORTUNITIES

At the clinic, we see patients every day. Some are not too sick with just a cold and other patients have some very serious conditions. However, no matter what their physical ailment is, we all suffer spiritually; even those who have a personal relationship with our Heavenly Daddy. There is a huge need for family stability in this culture. We are very blessed with our clinic staff who are strong Christians and are not ashamed to speak about the love of God. Ana Maria (my right hand and secretary) is not bashful and will speak with everyone about God and Jesus. She has helped so many of our patients through her prayers, talking with the patients and ministering to them with the gifts that God has given her. Wendy, our full time doctor, pastors a church in the evenings and has a pastoral heart. Often, a patient will go in to see Wendy to have a medical consult and come out an hour later. It is not that the medical needs are that great but the spiritual needs are that great. Wendy, like Ana Maria, will not hesitate to talk to our patients about their spiritual lives, talk with them, counsel them and pray with them. It is such an honour to serve God with these two amazing ladies as we treat the physical needs of our patients, but more important, treat their spiritual needs as well.

"Seek the Lord while he may be found; call on him while he is near."

Isaiah 55:6

January 12, 2010

Haiti Earthquake

It is January 12, 2010, 4:53 pm. I am working in the kitchen, Paul is working in his workshop and the kids are having some down time. Life is going on as normal. I finish preparing the dinner, call the family to wash up and we sit down for dinner. We say grace and start to eat when the cell phone rings. We usually do not answer the phone during dinner but something made me get up to answer it. It was my best friend Kim. *"Did you feel that?" "Feel what? I ask. 'THE EARTHQUAKE!!!! Things fell off our walls, everything shook. Everyone around here are outside their homes."* We had not felt a thing. Later, we would say that we did not feel the quake because Paul built us a good, strong house on a rock.

We turned on the computer and television to check the news. *Breaking News – 7.0 Earthquake hits Haiti. Undetermined number of people are dead, injured and buried.* We go to talk to our neighbours. They felt the quake and had cupboards open and pictures tilt on their walls. As the evening progressed, and more news was making it out of Haiti, we learned just how devastating this quake would turn out to be. It is said that about 3.5 million people were affected by this quake in Haiti. That about 220,000 people died and over 300,000 were injured. The quake left over 1.5 million people homeless.

The evening of quake, our phone started to ring off the hook from people looking for help and wanting to help. One call that we received was from the governing board of Haiti Children's Home, where we adopted our children from. They were trying to get communication to the orphanage to find out if they were okay. Once communication was made, it was discovered that the orphanage building was damaged but that no one was injured. Praise God! A day or two after the quake, the Haitian government, as well as other governments, announced that they would allow all Haitian children who were in the middle of being adopted, just waiting on paperwork, to have leave Haiti and go to their new adoptive families. The Canadian and US governments worked tirelessly to help get out as many about to be adopted Haitian children as possible. Both governments even sent planes just to airlift these children out of Haiti and take them to Canada and the USA. However, in order for these children to leave Haiti, some paperwork needed to be done. On the Haiti side, orphanages had to provide photos and some minimal documentation for each child before they could get a visa to go to Canada or the USA.

Patty, the Canadian contact for the orphanage, contacted me to ask for help. There was no internet in Haiti after the earthquake and they needed to get this paperwork done as soon as possible in order to get the children out of Haiti in the time frame that governments had given. Patty had a copy of all the kids' pictures and paperwork in Canada. She said that she could send it to me if I could forward it to the Embassies and various places in the DR that needed it. In 2010, internet in the DR very slow. Our internet connection was done via the cell phone towers and it was slow. We compared it with

1980's dial up speed. Patty spent many hours emailing me all
the photos and documents that were needed and giving me
the instructions of what to send where. It took a long time to
download all the files, especially the photos. I honestly did not
sleep for two days and worked on this almost non-stop for 48
hours. After three very long days, between Patty and I, we were
able to get all photos and documents where they needed to get
to for all the children that were eligible to fly out of Haiti and
go to their forever homes and families in the USA or Canada.

During these three days, I was also receiving and answering
emails from literally all over the world. Everything from friends
and families wanting to know if we were okay and what was
going on to strangers wanting to know how they could help.
We are members of Missionary Services Canada (MSC) and
Christian Missions in Many Lands (CMML) in the United
States. (MSC and CMML are affiliated together.) CMML
contacted us to say that they had already received a large sum
of donations from people wanting to help the people of Haiti.
It was quickly discovered that we were the only missionaries the
MSC and CMML had on this island. They asked if we would
help to distribute the donations and serve to help in Haiti. We
were already seeing how we could help but funds are always
such contributing factor as to how much one can help. After
talking details, CMML started to send us the donated funds
that they CMML and MSC had received for Haiti Relief. In
just a matter of a couple weeks, we were sent over $100,000US
for Haiti relief.

We spent time in prayer asking God to show us where and
how he wanted these amazing funds used to help His people.

One obvious area was Haiti Children's Home. They lacked all basic necessities for the children and staff. They had no clean water, food or even shelter. The United Nations came by about a week after the earthquake and provided a very large tent for the orphanage. We were in contact with the orphanage and were able to get needs list of what they really needed in the ways of food, medicine, soap and things such as diapers, blankets, towels, etc.

We went into the supermarket and talked with the owner to explain that we wanted to make a large purchase of food to take to Haiti. We did the same with the owner of the pharmacy that we always used. Both owners were so generous. Not only did they give us discounts, they also donated quite a bit, trusting us to take it to the orphanage. It truly is amazing how God opened so many doors and so many heart. God made collecting donations and buying large quantities so easy.

Next, how to get it all to Haiti. We were talking about how we would get everything to the orphanage when our phone rang. It was a missionary friend from another part of the country. He was calling to ask if we knew anyone who needed to take anything into Haiti because he had a friend who was going and had 90% of his truck empty. WOW. We said that we did and we could fill his truck. God put all the right people together at the right time. Within two days, over $10,000 of purchased food and items as well as more in donated items were on their way to the orphanage. The local businesses even donated things like toys for the children as they said that the children will need comfort and teddy bears and toys help to comfort children.

With all the centuries of racism between Dominican and Haitians, if you had told me on January 10th that on that following Sunday, Dominicans would fill churched and be on their knees praying for the country and people of Haiti, I never would have believed you. However, that is exactly what happened on the Sunday after the earthquake. Churches all over the Dominican Republic were overfilling and people were dropping to their knees to pray for Haitians and the country of Haiti. The Dominican government had trucks crossing the border into Haiti to bring in food, water and shelter less than 24 hours after the earthquake. They were the first country to respond and the last country to leave. The Dominican government opened the borders between the country, not charging any taxes, no visas were required and it took less time than stopping at a red light to cross back and forth between the two countries. The Dominican government kept the border open like this for about six months after the earthquake before going back to the "normal" ways for crossing the border.

Over the course of the next few months, we made numerous trips over to the orphanage to bring in food and other necessitates. We were able to do this only because of the very donations of so many people whom we do not know who generously gave through MSC Canada and CMML. Words will never be able to sufficiently describe our gratitude or the gratitude of the many Haitians who were helped in those first few months after the earthquake.

One day, Dominican missionary friends were over for a dinner and we were talking about how we were taking food and supplies over to the orphanage in Haiti. They mentioned how they had been trying to a help Haitian pastor that they knew up in the north. Pastor Eddy lives just across the border in Haiti in a town called Ouanaminthe. Prior to the earthquake, Pastor Eddy pastored a small church of about 200 people and they had started a feeding program to help out children who did not get enough food. They would cook the main meal for about 400 children once a week. Since the earthquake, his church had grown to over 1000, with about 600 refugees who had no family in the area to stay with. They were also now trying to provide one main meal a day to over 1000 people. Day after day, the trusted to Lord for food to cook and basic medical supplies.

After our friends told us about Pastor Eddy, we prayed about helping him and felt to Lord opening this door. Over the next few months, we made four trip to Pastor Eddy and his church. We took thousands of dollars of food, medical supplies and clothing to him and his rapidly growing congregation of refugees. Pastor Eddy is a very quiet, humble man. He thanked us over and over for the help. He invited Paul to preach at his church on Sunday so we planned a trip to bring more supplied and stay for church. Paul, through tri-lingual translation, preached to Pastor Eddy's congregation. It was an amazing and humbling afternoon. In Haiti, church services are usually four hours or longer and Pastor Eddy's church was no exception.

Since the earthquake, Pastor Eddy now pastors eight churches, has a school and a full time feeding program. God took this basic needs to we were humbled to help with and grew it. Pastor Eddy remains such a humble man and he is helping thousands of people. Not only is Pastor Eddy helping to provide practical needs, but more important, he is a vessel for God and being used to help with the spiritual needs of his entire flock. We are so blessed to have Pastor Eddy in our lives as he has taught us many things about taking care of one's flock.

June 2010

June Haiti Trips

I did not realize it has been so long since I updated the blog. The past six weeks have been busy. We have had ten different sets of guests in our house and we enjoyed them all. Some of have been friends we have not seen for many years and others we have seen recently. Anny's sponsors came and attended her grade 8 graduation and met her for the first time - which was great. The kids finished school and passed to the next grade levels. We are very proud of them. The kids also went to a ten day Kings Kids camp hosted by YWAM. For those of you who have been part of our support team all these years, you may remember back a number of years that we use to lead Kings Kids in the DR for six years with YWAM. It is amazing to think that now, our kids attend Kings Kid. Are we really getting older? Ummmmm......

In June, we made two trips to Haiti Children's Home. The first one was a very quick trip and made even quicker by border crossing problems which caused the team to spend the night on the DR side of the border. This cut their time at the orphanage down by an entire day. The team was a group from Santiago, led by missionaries from there who run a leadership program for Dominican young adults. They went to the orphanage to paint some fun stuff on the walls of the temporary building and do a lot of loving and playing with the orphans. It was a great couple days and everyone benefitted!

The second trip was from 17 - 21 June and it was another all men's building team. This time, the guys built a second temporary building, much like the first but a bit smaller. This building is housing the staff and volunteers and for the first time since the earthquake, on June 21st, they were not sleeping in tents and in the dirt. Praise God!

The enemy really did not want this trip to happen. One of the Dominican men who was supposed to go on this trip cut his hand with a table saw five days before the trip. We praise God that Marcos will heal and that he did not lose any fingers but he was not able to go on the trip. Two other Dominican men, who had not had work for a while, got new jobs a couple days before the trip and, therefore, we not able to go. The night before the trip, one of the men was not going to go as they had no food in the house and he could not go to Haiti and leave his wife with no food or money. However, God provided and food showed up at their door and he was able to go. In the end, five men went. Three from our Dominican church and two who flew in from Victoria Canada (Friendship Community Church) to go to Haiti and build this housing.

Two days before the trip, Paul was doing some last minute errands in town when our vehicle would not start. Then he saw smoke coming from under the hood. There was a short a small fire burning. He was able to put the fire out, make the repairs and there was no permanent damage. The next day, the clutch in the pickup truck started to act funny. Again, it was nothing. The morning that the team was leaving, the coffee pot got a short and stopped working and our washing machine would not do the spin cycle. Needless to say, we were feeling very attacked by the enemy but we know that God always wins.

The guys had safe travels, worked very hard in very hot conditions and accomplished the job God had for them. The guys were so hot and the humidity so high that in the middle of the afternoon, the guys took off their t-shirts and, literally, could ring out all the sweat from the shirts. They did work in evening hours, taking breaks in the afternoon as it was just too hot to work in the afternoons and much cooler to work once the sun set. The biggest distraction for the team was the adorable kids who want to play and help out as best as they can.

The workers at the orphanage have hard work as they do their very best to care for these 35 orphans while living in substandard housing with very little provisions in one of the poorest countries of the world. However, the faith that is so prevalent at the orphanage is amazing. God is everywhere. And not just at the orphanage but everywhere in Haiti! We are still hearing reports of God's name being raised in the streets of Haiti every single day. People are still turning away from voodoo and towards God. God is still winning the battles in Haiti.

As time goes on, Haiti is out of the news and we all can forget but please remember to pray for Haiti. Pray for the basic needs of the people. The government has closed their doors and are no longer receiving aid as their warehouses are full. This is so sad as the warehouses are full and the people are not receiving any of this aid. The people are starving, literally, and the government has buildings full of donated food that is not being distributed. The housing needs in Haiti will be huge for years to come. Rebuilding cannot be done quick enough and so many, many people are still homeless, living in tents or under sheets.

Keep praying the spiritual needs of the country and for all the relief workers, no matter who they are working with. The relief workers are exhausted. Some are Christian and some are not. Pray that the Christians are a testimony and light to the non-Christian relief workers and that all the people (Haitians and relief workers) see the light and love of Jesus shine through all the Christians.

Also, pray for the government. This government needs a lot of prayer and direction from our Lord. It is the only way that Haiti will recover.

Thank you everyone who has sent in a financial donation to help our work in Haiti. It is only because of your generosity that we are able to make these trip to Haiti and do the work we are doing there. In July, we plan to go to Northern Haiti to build a kitchen for church. This church is making hundreds and hundreds of meals each week for children and refugees from the earthquake who have moved North. The church as no kitchen and makes all these meals on an open campfire.

July 2010

Haiti Echos Mission Magazine Article

It has been just over seven months since a 7.0 rocked Port au Prince, Haiti at 4:53 pm. The world was in shock as pictures of the destruction, death or horrors of personal suffering hit the airwaves in the weeks that followed. Everyone heard about people who lost their lives, their families, homes, jobs, their children, everything! Even today, all these months later, there are still hundreds of thousands of Haitians living under bed sheets in the parks in and about Port au Prince and over 100,000 new orphans. Many others have fled to other parts of the country yet they still have no shelter, food or work. So much money, food and aid have been sent to or promised to the people of Haiti yet not a lot is actually getting into the hands of the people who need the help. Last month, the Haitian government said they are no longer accepting food donations as their warehouses are full. My question was "Why are the warehouses full when the people are starving?" There has always been corruption in the Haitian government and from what we have experienced, there has not been much change in this area. We have listened as many have voiced how they do not understand how Port au Prince is still a city of rubble with not much change as far as clean up and rebuilding goes. Haiti has always been one of the poorest, undeveloped countries in the world. Before the January earthquake hit Haiti, there was no real infrastructure in the country. How can anyone rebuild after such a huge natural disaster when there is no previous infrastructure to fall back on.

If the capital city of any developed country was 100% demolished in an earthquake or destroyed in floods, it would take time and money but the city, and country would rebuild. Seven months later, there would be significant change and improvement. A lot of this would be due in part to the fact that a developed country already has an established and functioning infrastructure. Haiti has never had this.

We heard how the Haitian people were and still are desperate but what is "desperate"? Can you truly understand what desperate is? Have you ever been hungry? Have you ever gone for an entire week without any food, not even a piece of gum? Have you watched your young children curl up in a ball and cry because their tummies hurt from starvation? Watched your child go litheless as they dehydrate because no one has had even one single drop of water for two days? Finally, an aid truck approaches and you run, you push people, you hit as you crawl up the side of the truck, doing everything that you can to get even one 8 oz. bottle of water. Then you rejoice as if you just won the $50 million lottery because you have a bottle of water in your hand - the first water you have seen or touched in days. You will do anything to get a drop of water into your child's mouth. We all saw the scenes on the news of Haitians grabbing and pushing at aid trucks and made comments as to their "bad and ungrateful behaviour". However, wouldn't you act the same way if you and your children had not had food for a week or water for days? You would do anything to survive. This is what

Haiti is like. This is what so many third world countries are like when a natural disaster hits. This is what is now happening in Pakistan with the massive floods and what will happen in any country when there is a catastrophic disaster.

We have listened as many people have said that God has forsaken Haiti. It always bothers me to hear this because the God that I know does not forsake His children. We, His children, have been blessed by God with free choice and the choices that us humans make are not always Godly choices. Hundreds of years ago, Haiti publicly dedicated their country to the practices and religion of voodoo. Today, they officially declare that their two official religions are Catholicism and voodoo. When the government of a country is publicly practicing voodoo, praying to satan, having satanic sacrifices and rituals, there is not a lot of room left for God to bless the country.

We must remember that not all Haitians believe and practice what is officially their country's religion. There are more Haitian Christians today than ever before in their history. Haiti has had more missionaries per capita than any other country. The Word of God is in Haiti and it is practiced!!!

In the weeks following the earthquake, once the sun set and there was no electricity, no homes left standing and the people were just wondering about on what was left of the streets of Port au Prince with nothing to do, no radio, no television, no social event, no church, no home, no food, no water - there was only one sound that was heard night after night. That was the sound of the Haitian people, signing out in their beautiful language of Creole, praises to God. The volume in the streets as God's name was lifted high was amazing. You did not hear the voodoo drums after dark. You heard praise and worship songs, prayers, and the Haitians glorifying God during these dark and difficult days.

One month after the earthquake, the Haitian government hosted a public memorial service to remember all those who died in the quake. This took place in downtown Port au Prince at the National Park. Thousands and thousands attended. One missionary wrote that as she was leaving the park after the service, she turned the corner and saw the house of one of the most famous voodoo witch doctors in Haiti. The house was still standing even though those around it was not. The witch doctor had a huge sheet on the ground and was digging up various idols and other items of his religion. The people had stopped to watch and were asking him "witch doctor, what are you doing." He stopped, looked at the crowd and announced, "none of these things work. Voodoo is all a lie. It cannot protect or help us. The only truth is God and we must all turn from our voodoo ways and follow God". WOW What a powerful testimony?

As parents of two adopted Haitian children living in the Dominican Republic, we have experienced firsthand the very real and cruel prejudices that many Dominicans have towards their Haitian neighbours. We pulled our children out of the local school because the prejudices towards our children from other children were so intense that our one child was actually praying for God to change his skin colour so the kids would stop teasing him. Haitian children are commonly referred to by very crude racial slurs. With prejudices between these two countries going so deep and with so much terrible history over the centuries, if someone had told me on January 10th that Dominicans all over the country would be on their knees in most every church in the Dominican Republic praying for Haiti and all Haitians, I would have never believed it. Yet - that is exactly what happened on January 17th!!! All over the Dominican Republic, Dominicans were praying for their brothers and sisters on the other side of the island. Dominicans really stepped up and were generously giving to Haiti. We witnessed Dominicans who are very poor going through what little items they owned in their house in order to donate a t shirt, a cooking pot, a blanket - all with the attitude that the Haitians now had nothing, absolutely nothing yet the Dominicans still had a house over their head and their children were alive.

Two months after the earthquake, we took a work team of Dominican men from our Dominican church over to Haiti to build some temporary housing for an orphanage (Haiti Children's Home). Haiti Children's Home's (HCH) building was still standing but due to the twisting of the building that happened in the earthquake, the UN engineers condemned the building, saying that it had to be torn down. As a result, since the afternoon of the earthquake, 36 orphanages ages newborn to 10 plus nannies and staff had been sleeping outside in the dirt. This team of Dominican builders were nothing fancy. They were a group of men who, by world standards, are the poor that the missionaries are here to help. They have families, minimal income, live job to job, lack food, lack money for school supplies, etc. Yet these men have Jesus in their hearts and they wanted to help. With the generosity of people from Canada and the US who sent in financial donations, we were able to take this group of men over the HCH to build temporary housing for the orphans and staff. The men worked very hard in extreme heat (40C) from 5 am until midnight for three long days and built a 16'x48' plywood building that now houses all the orphans.

The following Sunday at church, the pastor asked this team of men to come forward, tell about their trip to Haiti, what they did and any testimonies. For each one of these men, it was their first time in Haiti. One man, through his tears, simple said "Compared to the children in Haiti, our children live like Kings and Queens". When the team was leaving HCH, one of the workers at HCH, a 21-year-old Haitian man who was orphaned himself and raised at HCH told the Dominican men that he never liked Dominicans because his whole life he had heard nothing but bad things about them. He had never met a Dominican before in his life but now, he has five new brothers in Christ, they just happen to be Dominicans.

The earthquake, as tragic as it was, has opened many spiritual doors. Haitians have been accepting Jesus in their hearts, Dominicans' hearts have changed and they now see the Haitians as their brothers and sisters. There has been a spiritual revival happening, not just in Haiti, but on this entire island since January 12, 2010, when the ground shook, the idols fell and God was raised up on high!

July 2010

Excerpt from Our Newsletters

EVANGELISTIC CRUSADE IN PEDREGAL!!!

August 16th is a day that we would like to ask prayer for. We are hosting an evangelistic crusade in Pedregal. August 16th is a national holiday so there will be a lot of people about. We are working with a number of local churches to put on this crusade with different churches taking different roles. One church will do worship, one will do the prayers, etc. We are bringing up a local Dominican crusade preacher from Santo Domingo and Paul is also going to be speaking.

There has been a lot of spiritual battles going on in Pedregal lately and we just really feel that God is saying that now is the time to do a large scale evangelistic crusade. We are so thankful for the local Dominican Christians who are helping us to organize and put on this crusade. Your prayers not only for us but for all those involved in putting on the crusade and for all those who will be hearing to Word and Love of God on August 16th are appreciated!

Library

There is such a hunger in the Dominican Christians for reading more about Christian growth and other various books. Books here are very expensive. For example, Rick Warren's "Purpose driven Life" sells for $38 whereas I can buy it off amazon.com for about $5. We would like to acquire numerous Spanish Christian books and begin a library at the clinic. If you would like to donate any Spanish books or funds to help purchase or make a purchase and post it to us, please let us know. Right now, we only have about 15 books to put into a library and there are so many good books available out there. If you happen to have any Spanish books in your home or wherever and would like to send them to us, that would great. It does not matter if a book is new or used, just as long as it has it all the pages.

January 2011

Excerpt from Our Newsletters

Wednesday marks the One Year Anniversary of the Haiti Earthquake. One later and the scenes in and around Port au Prince are not too much different than they were in the weeks following the quake. Presidential elections took place in November with no result and a new vote between the top two candidates is suppose to take place in January. However, there is still dispute as to who the top two candidates are. On Wednesday, Paul will travel to the Haiti/Dominican border to deliver an industrial stove, 100 lb propane tank and kitchen cabinets to Pastor Eddy. Before the quake, our friend and Haitian Pastor, Eddy had two churches, an orphanage with about 15 kids and a weekly feeding program feeding about 50 children. Now, he has nine churches, about 65 orphans and feeds about 150 children and refugees daily. He is an amazing pastor, loves his people and is giving his life to serve God and his people in Haiti. We are so thankful to all those who donated and made it possible to provide Pastor Eddy and his church with a functional kitchen with which to cook all these meals with. We have also equipped the kitchen with many groceries to help feed the people. God is moving powerfully in Haiti and many are still giving their hearts and lives over to God, turning away from the traditional voodoo ways of Haiti. Praise God and God alone!!!!

Sharyn Branson

We are also sponsoring a house for a refugee family in the Port au Prince area. We are not actually building the house but providing the funds. We have partnered with friends of ours and their ministry called NET (Nations in Transformation). They have been operating a camp for 50 families ever since the earthquake and are now getting houses built for the families. This week they are getting materials cleared through Customs, with the help of Samaritans Purse and at the end of January, with a team from a church in Michigan, will begin building these pre-fabricated homes. With funds that many have donated to us for Haiti, we are sponsoring one entire house for a family who has been living in a tent for a year now. We will send pictures of the house when we receive them.

On the Dominican side of the border - we have our first mission team arriving from North Carolina on January 22 and are looking forward to what God will do through them and the lives that they will touch during their time here. Our next team is in March. The clinic continues to move along and we continue to wait on our Lord to open the doors of what HE wants done next. We are still waiting on confirmation of the land with church. The church is in the process of trying to borrow money to buy the land and then we can proceed to build the clinic on their land. Prayers for God's will and clear direction are appreciated.

"*Every word of God is flawless; he is a shield to those who take refuge in him.*"

Proverbs 30:5

April 2011

Excerpt from Our Newsletters

Witnessing Miracles

Day after day our time is filled with seeing patients, praying for people, building something, planting something, communicating around the world, updating, accounting, home schooling, cooking, cleaning..... and the days fly by. Recently, everyone within our ministry has been focusing more on what God is saying is important. Things like the days starting with staff devotions, taking the time to really listen to those who come for counsel, prayer, fellowship. Through this, we are honoured to witness miracles. We are seeing one family who fell from the Lord growing closer to our Lord as they depend more on His strength and not their own. As a result, there is now employment and a means to buy food for the family. A mother is fighting cancer, third time out of remission and given grave news from the doctors. She is now bouncing around the village as God has once again put her into remission. Students who have not being doing their best in school now focusing, bringing home great report cards and they are giving all the credit only to God! It is such an honour to be a part of the miracles and the works of our Father in Heaven!

13 – 21 July 2011

Eduardi

"It hurts. I can to see!"

It is 6 am and Ana Maria is abruptly woken by her husband, Eduardi, yelling that it hurts and he cannot see and then he collapses on the bed. Ana Maria does not know what is happening. She yells for her sons. One son runs next door to get help. Ana Maria cannot wake Eduardi. She has no idea what is going on. Family who live next door come running into the house. They pick up Eduardi, put him in his nephew's car, who then drives Eduardi and Ana Maria to the public hospital.

It is now about 6:30 am, I am waking up as we have a mission team of 20 people in country and a busy day ahead. My phone rings. A very upset and frantic Ana Maria is speaking so fast that I can hardly understand her. I hear "Eduardi", "not waking up", "hospital". I talk calmly and get Ana Maria to catch her breath. She then explains what has happened. She says that the hospital has Eduardi lying on a Gurney in the hallway and no one is doing anything. He is still unconscious and has yet to open his eyes. I tell Ana Maria that we must get Eduardi down to the next city, La Vega, where there are private clinics and better medical care than up in our little area. Ana Maria said that they do not have the money. I tell her that money does not matter, Eduardi is very sick and we need to get him better care immediately. I say that we will take care of the costs and trust God to provide. We do not have money for medical costs, transport, etc. but I know that money does not matter right now. Eduardi's life and doing all that we can do is what matters at this moment.

Ana Maria calls me back about twenty minutes later. They have an ambulance and they are about to leave for La Vega. "Good", I say. "Be sure to take Eduardi to the private clinic, not the public hospital." I tell Ana Maria again not to worry about money - we will help and God will provide. God knew that this was going to happen today and He already has a way to take care of everything - no matter what happens. Ana Maria is scared. I try to comfort her over the phone. I tell her to call when she gets to La Vega.

I get up out of bed. Paul has already risen and starting to wake the kids. I am suppose to home school the kids this morning while Paul heads out to work with the team. I have a feeling that this is not going to be normal day. Paul and I decide that we will all join the team breakfast and the kids will have a day off school. As the kids are getting ready, I grab a few things for school that the kids can do at the ministry site. We head out the door to the camp where the mission team is staying and have breakfast. We share with the team about Eduardi and Ana Maria and spend a bit of time in prayer. We all then head into Pedregal for a day of ministry.

When we arrive in Pedregal, I go to my clinic to check on things and see what coverage I need as Ana Maria will not be working today. I send word to our back up secretary, Juana, asking her if she can work today. When Juana arrives, I ask if she is available for the next few days as I have a feeling that Ana Maria will not be working.

It about 8:30 am and I go outside for some privacy to call Ana Maria. Ana Maria is frantic. The ambulance took them to the public hospital and just dropped them at the entrance to the ER and left. Eduardi is lying in the hallway and no medical person has seen him. Ana Maria did tell me that a doctor on his way out of the hospital, stopped, took a two second look at Eduardi and said that he needed to be seen immediately by a specialist. I told Ana Maria to get an ambulance and immediately take Eduardi to the private clinic. Eduardi was still unconscious. I did not want to scare Ana Maria but I knew that things were very critical for Eduardi. I told Ana Maria that Eduardi could die right there, lying on that Gurney in the hallway of the public hospital. He must get to the private clinic to have any hope of surviving.

In the meantime, I am trying to figure out how I can get down to La Vega to help Ana Maria. I want to be there to help her, support her, help her get the care Eduardi needs and help Ana Maria make the medical decisions. Before I can go to La Vega, I have to make sure that everything is okay at the clinic as patients are already showing up and looking for their help and treatment. Wendy, our ministry doctor, says that she will take care of all things at the clinic today so Ana Maria nor I have to worry about the clinic. Good - clinic is taken care of.

Next is the mission team. During the day, I usually do not have a lot to do with the team as Paul handles all the construction and evangelism ministry. The team has their lunch and Nena will have dinner ready for the team, just like she always does. I call her to ensure that she does not need anything and she assures me that she will handle everything in regards to the team's food for the day.

Next is my children. Paul is busy with the team and I cannot take them to the clinic in La Vega. Not only will they be so bored, children are not allowed in the ICU and other areas of the clinic. Anny, our foster daughter is in school all day so she cannot help. One of the ladies on the mission team comes up to me and asks if she could help me by taking care of my kids for the day. The kids would hang with the team, Paul will be there the entire time but she will watch over my kids, make sure that they are helping, entertained, out of trouble, fed, drink water, etc. so that I can go to Ana Maria. Wow - what a blessing. I go talk to Paul. He is so supportive and tells me to go. Call him when I get to La Vega and then call with updates. The whole team is understanding and says a prayer as I depart, leaving the team, to go to Ana Maria.

When I get to La Vega and to the private clinic that Eduardi is now at, I find Ana Maria upstairs, outside of the ICU. When she sees me, she throws her arms around me, crying, and praising God for Him taking care of Eduardi. Ana Maria tells me that the neurologist is examining Eduardi and then they are going to do a CAT scan. Eduardi still is unconscious. Ana Maria then tells me that she almost collapsed when the neurologist came in to examine Eduardi. He is the same doctor who stopped to look at Eduardi in the hallway of the public hospital and said that he needed a specialist right away. We sat and waited while the neurologist did his examination and then came out to talk to Ana Maria.

Ana Maria introduced me to Dr. Reyes and told him who I was. Dr. Reyes explained that he believed that Eduardi had suffered a stroke but would be waiting for the CAT scan before making a final diagnosis. Eduardi was breathing on his own. Eduardi just turned 51 years old, does not smoke or drink, is healthy, and strong. He works as a welder and keep fit through his work. A bit later, Eduardi is taken for the scan.

About thirty minutes later, Dr. Reyes asks Ana Maria and I to join him in his office. Dry Reyes explains that the scan confirms that Eduardi has had a stroke. It is very serious and Dr. Reyes does not give any definite prognosis. For now, he will keep Eduardi in the ICU, he has an IV and receiving various medications that will hopefully help to reduce the swelling. Eduardi is also getting IV antibiotics to help prevent pneumonia. As this is a private clinic, Dr. Reyes also has to talk about payment. He explains that for right now, he is lower his fees so as that the family can use whatever limited resources that they have to pay for the ICU care and medications. We are grateful for this. However, it will still cost about $800 a day to keep Eduardi in the clinic. There is no decision to make - it is this or Eduardi will definitely die. Ana Maria and I say a prayer and ask for God's provision. I tell her that I will use my credit card to make the first payment so that there is no interruption in the medical care that Eduardi so desperately needs right now. As I walk down the stairs to the administration office, I thank God that we have a credit card that we never use, keeping the balance at zero with idea that we will never use this card unless there is an emergency. Today is such an emergency. I have no idea how we will pay the credit card bill..... but God does.

By the time that I get back upstairs to the ICU waiting room, it is about 4 pm. Ana Maria's mother and aunt have arrived, as well as Eduardi and Ana Maria's children (Katherine, Oluarvi, and Cristian). Ana Maria is on the phone with their oldest son, Owaldy, who is at college in the United States. Ana Maria thrusts the phone into my hand and, through her tears, asks me to explain to Owaldy what is happening with Eduardi. It is a tough phone conversation as I explain to a son that his dad is very sick. Owaldy asks if his dad could die from this. I have to be honest and say that it is possible but also that no one knows what will happen. Anything can happen.

The rules for the ICU are that family can spend fifteen minutes at a time with the patient, four times a day. That is it. The fifteen minute visits have to be shared with by the loved ones and only two people are allowed in the ICU at a time. I had already been in a few times to see Eduardi and Dr. Reyes said that I could go in and out as often as I wanted. Ana Maria would decide who went in on each visit. First, their children. It was tear-wrenching to watch the kids go in, one at a time, with Ana Maria to see their dad. They each left the ICU in tears, collapsing into my arms or the arms of their Grandma or Aunt. The next, and last ICU visit of the day, would not be allowed until 8pm. Ana Maria was sitting right beside in the waiting area. I gave some money to one of our friends who had shown up and asked him to go buy some bottles of water, pop and food as Ana Maria had not eaten all day. Ana Maria's friend, Julia, had been with Ana Maria from her house at 6 am until now and said that she would stay the night at the clinic with Ana Maria. I made sure that they had what they needed for the night before I headed back up the mountain.

I arrived at the camp just as dinner with the team was finishing up. Nena had done another fantastic meal and had saved a plate for me. I did not realize how hungry I was; but then I had not eaten since breakfast and it was now almost 7 pm. Everyone had questions so before I ate, I stood in front of the team and gave them all an update on Eduardi and Ana Maria. It was now a waiting game to see how or if Eduardi would respond to the medicine and wake up. The first 24 hours are the most critical. We were at about hour thirteen. The team all prayed, right then and there, for Eduardi, Ana Maria, their family and Dr. Reyes.

Paul, Nena and I talked while I ate. We all decided that I would head back down to La Vega to help Ana Maria in the morning. Nena would watch over our kids while hanging out with the team for the day. The team was also fabulous and they offered to help out in any way that they could, including with our kids. There was no shortage of help for anyone.

People in Pedregal had all rallied around Ana Maria and her family. This is very Dominican. When there is a need, everyone tries to help. Dinner was waiting for Ana Maria's children when they returned home from La Vega that night. Their Grandma, Katherine and her husband, Fernandito, all stayed at the house for the night. They all slept together on the floor in the living room/dining room area - not one of them wanting to be alone during this very hard night. Ana Maria promised to call if anything changed during the night.

The next morning, before I even got out of bed, I called Ana Maria to see how the night went. There was no change yet. After getting my family up and ready for the day, Paul headed to the team with the kids while I headed down the mountain to Ana Maria. Ana Maria asked to me come before 8:00 am, if I could, as Dr. Reyes was going to be assessing Eduardi and she wanted me there to help her understand the medical lingo and make decisions.

The enemy does not like it when God's people are doing His work for His glory and, as so many of God's children were pulling together to do their part to help, the enemy was plotting. I drove down our road and had just turned onto the main road that would take me down the mountain to La Vega when smoke started to come out the back of my SUV and the vehicle started to sputter and lost all power. I was able to complete my turn and pull over. I called Paul and told him what happened. Paul could not come to help as he had the kids and the mission team. Daniel, one of our ministry staff, came with the mechanic, Rafi. Rafi did a quick assessment, said that the vehicle was good to drive to his shop. Once at the shop, Rafi said that the turbo had gone and would need to be replaced before I could drive the vehicle again. Augh - what timing. I needed to get to La Vega, Paul need the truck for the team, we had so much on the go at this time. I could not be a week without a vehicle. After talking with Paul and saying a prayer, we decided to rent a vehicle. Renting vehicles in the DR is not cheap and you have basically no liability coverage so this is not our first choice but, at this time, we had no choice.

I walked down to the car rental place, which thankfully was about 200 m down the road from Rafi's mechanic shop. They had one vehicle available to rent.... only one. Praise God, I only needed one! After about thirty minutes, I had the vehicle rented and was on my way down to La Vega. I arrived at the clinic, ran up to the fourth floor and found Ana Maria in the ICU waiting area. She said that Dr. Reyes had an emergency come into the ER so he had not been there yet to assess Eduardi. About ten minutes later, Dr. Reyes arrived. Once again, the enemy tried to stop things but God kept everything under control and it all turned out just fine.

After taking time to assess Eduardi, see his latest stats, blood work, etc., we went to his office to talk about Eduardi's treatment. Dr. Reyes was very honest and told Ana Maria that it has been 24 hours and no change in Eduardi's condition. They had determined that Eduardi was now blind; a result of the stroke, and, at this time, partially paralyzed. Eduardi had no spontaneous response to pain, light or stimuli. Eduardi had not opened his eyes or shown any signs of consciousness since arriving at the clinic 24 hours earlier. At this time, the only thing that we could do was wait, keep up the medications and pray. No one can predict the outcome at this time.

We shared with Dr. Reyes the day before how we were all Christians and believed in the will and power of God. If it is God's will to heal Eduardi, then He will. If God chooses not heal Eduardi, then it is because God has a greater reason for what is happening to Eduardi and his family. However, it was going to be a long day.

I called Paul and told him the latest news after our talk with Dr. Reyes. Eduardi is a good friend of Paul's and it pains him to hear of his friend's condition, and also that he is not able to be at the clinic right now. Ana Maria is my best friend. This case is not just about helping someone that our ministry has contact with. This is personal. This our good friends.

Ana Maria has always amazed me with her strong faith in God. However, during Eduardi's illness, I saw that Ana Maria has the strongest faith in God of any person that I know. Ana Maria has taught me so much and I can only hope to be half the child of God as she was during Eduardi's illness.

Eduardi stayed in a coma for the next several days. During these days, Eduardi's family only were able to be at his bedside four times a day for fifteen minutes at a time. In the ICU were three other beds and every bed held a patient. During Ana Maria's fifteen minutes in the ICU, she would take time to share about God to the other patients and their families. Over the next five days, Ana Maria led four people to the Lord. Three were patients, two of which passed on within hours of asking Jesus into their hearts. Praise God! The other person was a family member of one of the patients. It still amazing me how Ana Maria had the strength, in the midst of her own sorrow, to take precious time away from being with her husband of 24 years to share about God and lead others to accept Jesus into their lives.

Meanwhile, back home in Pedregal, everyone was doing what they could help. Family and neighbours were helping to feed Ana Maria's son, sending food to the hospital for her, watching over the boys, cleaning her house, etc. I would often have family members or friends coming along with me as I drove to La Vega to see Ana Maria and Eduardi every day.

At the same time, we had a mission team from Canada of 18 people who we were responsible for. The team was awesome and gave me so much grace for not being around them. Paul and Daniel lead the team and Nena was always there to cook and ensure the team was well fed. As the team worked on a house two doors down from Ana Maria's, Paul and the team would see and talk to many people who were coming by Ana Maria's house to ask how Eduardi was doing. During this time, Paul and some of the team members were able to share about God's faithful love to us all. While Eduardi was hospitalized, four more people accepted the Lord into their lives in Pedregal.

Eduardi's illness was the starting point to bring eight people to the Lord and ask Jesus into their hearts and for God to be their Father. It was truly amazing.

Six days later, the team was nearing the end of their time with us, Eduardi's physical had deteriorated and the medical bills were growing daily. Eduardi developed pneumonia and was now fighting fluid on his lungs and infection. He had yet to open his eyes in six days. Ana Maria made the hard decision to transfer Eduardi to the public hospital in Santiago. The hospital agreed to take Eduardi and, being that it is a hospital in the big city, they had the equipment and staff needed to managed Eduardi's care. However, before the clinic would release Eduardi for transfer to Santiago, the bill had to paid in full. It was over $5000. The leader of the mission team pulled me aside and said that they had an emergency fund for the team. Being that the team was leaving in two days and they had not needed the fund, they wanted to help Ana Maria with the clinic bill. They had been in touch with their home church it was already approved. The team leader went to the clinic with me that afternoon and between his emergency fund and my visa card, we paid the bill in full and got Eduardi transferred to Santiago.

We did not have the $2500 to pay our visa bill that we just put on the card. However, God had it and He is for faithful. Once word got out that this bill had to be paid and that we could not get Eduardi transferred without paying it, which is why we charged it to our visa card; people started to send in money to pay the visa bill. Within a week, the visa was paid in full with a bit of extra money sent to help Ana Maria with other expenses that she had in regards to Eduardi. God and His children are so amazing.

Eduardi's transfer in the ambulance from La Vega to Santiago went smoothly on a Monday afternoon, six days after the initial stroke. Eduardi was settled into the ICU and Ana Maria was at peace with the situation. So far, Ana Maria had not left Eduardi's side or the ICU.

We had our team leaving on Wednesday morning, another team arriving on Saturday and then we were leaving for two months in Canada and the USA two days after the second team leaves. It was a very busy time but Eduardi and Ana Maria took priority for us all. When I could not make it to Santiago, Ana Maria and I were talking on the phone four or five times a day.

Tuesday, Eduardi was peaceful but his condition did not change. He remained in a coma, fighting pneumonia but he was not in pain. Wednesday, Eduardi was in the same condition. Ana Maria was exhausted. We were encouraging her to go home for about 12 hours to rest but she would not leave Eduardi's side. At the Santiago hospital, Ana Maria continued to share about God to all who would listen; patients, family members, nurses, doctors, lab tech - everyone.

Wednesday night, at about 9 pm, I called Ana Maria. She was tired, a good friend was with her for the night, Eduardi had not changed. Eduardi's brother had come up from the Capital and was always with Ana Maria at the hospital. At about midnight, my phone rang. I knew in my gut that it was not going to be good. Ana Maria was crying, she said that Eduardi opened his eyes, looked right at her, smiled and then he gasped for breath and collapsed. Ana Maria tells me that there are four doctors plus nurses all around Eduardi's bed trying to keep him alive but that she thinks that this is it. I pray with her, then she tells me that she must go to Eduardi and hangs up. I sit up in bed, praying and waiting. Fifteen minutes later, the phone rings. All I hear is "Sharyn - he is gone. Can you come get us?"

It is now almost 1 am. It is very dangerous to drive the roads in the middle of the night but I knew that we must. However, it is even more dangerous for a single woman to drive the highways and mountain road in the middle of the night. Paul called a missionary friend of ours with the strange request if we could drop our kids off at their house right now and we will pick them up in the morning? Our friend said that his family was away, he was home alone so he will come over to our right away, sleep on our couch and be there for our kids. WOW - God is so good in how he orchestrates things ahead of time. We waited for our friend to show up as it took about fifteen minutes or so to drive from his house to our house, then we quietly left our house, so as not to wake our kids, and made the drive to Santiago.

We arrived at the ER at the Santiago hospital to find Ana Maria, Julia and Eduardi's family waiting for us outside. After hugs and tears, we piled into the vehicle to make the drive home and tell the kids that their Dad has died. It was a long hour drive home. We got to Ana Maria's house in Pedregal at about 4 am. As our vehicle drove into the village and headed to Ana Maria's house, lights started to come on in neighbours' houses. People knew that something had happened.

We got to the house; Ana Maria entered the house first. Her kids and son in law were all asleep, together, on the floor of the living room. We turned on the lights and started to wake everyone. No words were really spoken. Everyone knew right away that Eduardi had gone to glory. As the tears and cries started, the neighbours started to arrive.

The men pulled Paul aside as they asked for details and then started to do what the men do so well - whatever they could to fix what they could. First thing was to get Eduardi from the hospital and bring him home for the burial process. Men volunteered, vehicle was gotten, gas money pitched in and this small group of men headed down to Santiago to pick up their friend.

Ana Maria and I placed the hard call to Eduardi's and Ana Maria's oldest son, Owaldy. It was such a hard phone call.... to call a young man of only 23 who is geographically far away to tell him that his Daddy has gone heaven. More people pitched in to help and at 10 pm that very night, Paul, and Ana Maria's kids headed down for the 3-hour drive to the capital city airport to pick up Owaldy who arrived from the USA. Come 2 am, 24 hours after Eduardi went home to heaven, the family was all together.

In the Dominican culture, a body is brought to their home in a casket, the body is prepared right there. Family and friends come to the house to pay their respect and mourn. Dominicans are a people who do not hide their feelings. Wailing, crying, screams, whimpers were heard all day long. A blue tarp is put up in the front patio area. When you see the blue tarp, everyone knows that someone has died. The purpose of the tarp is to provide protection from the sun and rain while so many come to the house. Eduardi's family all arrived from different parts of the country; everyone except his Dad who was too ill to travel. Eduardi has six siblings and both his parents were still living.

A service was held around the casket on Thursday. Our staff pastors (Wendy Diaz and Pablo Almonte) conducted the service and it was perfect.

Ana Maria had not seen her oldest son for over a year, since he went to university in the US on scholarship. When Owaldy left, he was a kid, not serving the Lord much. After being able to spend a couple hours alone with Owaldy, Ana Maria shared with me that a boy left and a man of God returned home.

Owaldy was able to take on the role of man of the family after his dad passed.

It is now late on Thursday night. Ana Maria nor I have slept in two days. We are exhausted physically, and emotionally but not spiritually. God is giving us all strength every moment. Ana Maria and I had some precious moments alone during these days that were the worst in Ana Maria's life. Yet, Ana Maria's faith never faltered; it only grew stronger. I marveled at her faith and asked myself if I could be as spiritually strong as my dear friend. I learned so much from my friend during those weeks.

Friday morning was the day to bury Eduardi. In the Dominican Republic, people are not buried into the ground but put I tombs above ground. The ground is too hard to dig that deep and there is a space problem. Tombs that are large enough to fit a casket are built one on top of another up to six high. A friend of the family offered his family tomb space to Ana Maria for Eduardi. In seven years' time, she will have to either buy her own space or collect the casket and bones.

So many came to pay their respect to Eduardi and support his family. The trucks lined up. The casket was loaded into the back of Paul's pick up. People climbed into the vehicles and into the bed of trucks. My vehicle was reserved for Ana Maria and her immediate family. Some of her sons chose to ride with their Dad. The police had been notified and they were managing traffic as our convoy of various run down vehicles made the slow procession from Ana Maria and Eduardi's home to the cemetery, about 2 km away. It took about 25 minutes to make the drive.

Upon arriving at the cemetery, Eduardi is carried from the truck to a slab of concrete at the entrance where caskets are laid. A ceremony is held, prayers are said, and then Eduardi's sons, brothers and Paul carry the casket to the tomb at the back of the cemetery. The cemetery worker is waiting with mixed concrete. The casket is placed in the tomb and cement is paid to cover the hole to the tomb. With that, Eduardi is buried.

We return to Ana Maria's for the traditional meal that is hosted by the family for all who care to come. Friends and ladies of the village of taken on the task of preparing this meal. About two hundred people are there for the lunch. After lunch, as Ana Maria and I sit quietly off to one side, she whispers "I want the blue tarp taken down. It makes me very sad. Eduardi is not here. He is in Heaven." Dominican Catholic traditions dictates that the tarp is left up for ten days. Ana Maria wanted it down. It made her very sad. I went to Paul and told him this request. Within ten minutes, the men had the tarp down. Eduardi is in Heaven, not under the blue tarp.

Eduardi had lived a life not always for God. In his twenties, he came to the Lord through a preacher in the Capital. Eduardi served with this preacher for many years. Learning from him and growing in the Lord. Then one day, the preacher failed him. The preacher had an affair and left his wife and family. Eduardi had put more of his faith in this man than in God and as a result, when this man fell, so did Eduardi's faith. Eduardi never stopped Ana Maria nor his children from going to church, learning about God or being Christians but he made it clear that he was done with God.

Over the years, Eduardi and Paul had developed a good friendship. Paul considered Eduardi one of his better friends. The four of us all enjoyed each other friendship. One day, exactly two weeks before Eduardi's stroke, Paul and Eduardi were talking. Eduardi had shared about his faith, and lack of faith, with Paul over the years. On this particular day, Paul told Eduardi that he needed to forgive this preacher and put his faith in God not in any man. Eduardi and Paul talked a long time that day and Eduardi agreed. Together, they prayed and Eduardi forgave the preacher and asked God to come back into his life and heart. Eduardi had not shared this with anyone, including Ana Maria.

After Eduardi's stroke, before he passed, Paul was able to share this with Ana Maria and their kids. This was such an answered prayer and has given a lot of peace to those who have survived Eduardi. Through Eduardi's testimony, others also forgave and gave their lives to God; even though Eduardi was not able to verbally share his testimony.

God does use all things for good when we step out of the way and let Him lead and do His work.

"In God we make our boast all day long, and we will praise your name forever."

Psalm 44:8

November 2011

Ana Maria's Brain Tumor

Ana Maria has been complaining of swollen fingers, ankles and feet that were so swollen that they hurt. We tried reducing salt and increasing the water in her diet but that did not seem to help. We sent her to an endocrinologist to get her thyroid checked. Everything came back normal. For months, Ana Maria suffered from this swelling. Her face even seemed to be swollen and she was starting to get headaches. We decided to send her for a CAT scan. The CAT scan showed a tumour right behind her nose, at her frontal lobe, pressing on her optical nerves. This was discovered just two short months after Eduardi, her husband, died. It was devastating news. Ana Maria had her two youngest still at home, the entire family still very much grieving the loss of Eduardi and now, Ana Maria has a brain tumour. It was all very scary. However, Ana Maria's faith never faltered and she kept saying that there was a reason that God was allowing all this to happen to her and her family.

We started researching what treatment options were available to treat Ana Maria. At this time, we were not sure the type of tumour; if it was malignant or not. Ana Maria consulted with a neurosurgeon in the Capital city. He was the only surgeon in the country who could do the type of surgery that Ana Maria needed. He said that he could but he the only way that he could be able to get to the tumour would be cut Ana Maria's face and go in through the face to reach the tumour. In the United States we have friends in common with Ana Maria, and we shared Ana Maria's diagnosis. One of our friends started the ball rolling and it is so obvious how God was in total control from the first moment. Our friend, Liz, called a friend who called a friend who called a friend. Within a few weeks, someone had volunteered for Ana Maria to stay at her home, someone had contacted a hospital who agreed to waive the hospital fees, a surgeon and surgical staff volunteered their time to do the surgery and follow up, others spoke up to volunteer other needs. Due to the higher technology in the US, the surgeon says that he will use a scope through the nasal cavity to remove the tumour. He says that he will not be opening Ana Maria's face to get to the tumour. Praise God! Someone offered to pay Ana Maria's plane ticket. Everything was falling into place for Ana Maria to go to South Carolina to receive the surgery and treatment that she needed in order to survive. The tumour was rapidly growing and, if it was not removed, could kill her.

The one thing left, of which no one could volunteer or donate, was to obtain a US medical emergency visa for Ana Maria to enter the US and receive treatment. It is very hard for Dominicans to obtain a visa and the odds were against Ana Maria in obtaining such a visa. Ana Maria and I talked the day before she heads to the US embassy and we both agree that if it is God's will for her to go to the US for this treatment, then God will provide the visa. If she is denied the visa, then God has another plan. Letters were written by the surgeon, the hospital, a local church, etc. for Ana Maria to submit to the Embassy with her visa application. A call to prayer went out for all to pray for the application for Ana Maria. Ana Maria had her appointment with the embassy, her passport, application, letters and everything else that we knew to send her with. Due to the embassy rules, Ana Maria had to enter alone to apply for the visa.

As Ana Maria is inside the embassy, many are praying. Liz sits outside the embassy, waiting. A couple hours later, Ana Maria exits that embassy with an approved emergency medical visa. God's will be done. She is off to the US for her treatment. It was April 2012.

The very next day, Liz and Ana Maria board a plane for South Carolina. It is the first time that Ana Maria has ever left her country and the first time on an airplane. Not only that, she is leaving behind her two youngest children, in the care of her sister and mother, only a few short months after losing Eduardi, their father. Words can never describe the multitude of emotions that Ana Maria was experiencing as that plane took off from Santo Domingo to the United States.

I was not present during the next few months of Ana Maria's life but we were in constant contact via emails and phone calls. I will do my best to summarize what Ana Maria went through, but more important, tell how God used so many to help Ana Maria.

Friends from Georgia made contact with their denominational church in the Charleston area to ask for help for Ana Maria. Liz also used her contacts from growing up in Charleston to seek help for Ana Maria. A young couple offered for Ana Maria to live with them during her entire stay in Charleston, as well as to help get her to and fro for all her medical appointments and treatments. The wife is a nurse at the hospital where Ana Maria had her surgery, which was a blessing from God.

Ana Maria started with meeting the surgeon, having various consults, and tests performed in order to prepare her for surgery. The day before her surgery, her oldest son, who was studying on scholarship in Ohio, was able to fly down to Charleston and spend the next week with her. He was by her side before surgery, after surgery or those first few days of recovery. What a huge blessing to Ana Maria to have her son with her. She was blessed by so many brothers and sisters of Christ who were by her bedside, but having her son there was priceless. Thanks to the generosity of others who paid for her son's plane ticket, he was able to be with his Mom.

Ana Maria's surgery was scheduled for a Friday morning, about five months after her initial diagnosis and just under ten months since Eduardi had died. When I talked with her the night before her surgery, she was praising God for all these difficulties in her life. She was sharing her story with other patients and telling everyone about how good and faithful God is. Ana Maria is a constant example to me of how, no matter what happens in life, to never lose your faith in God but allow it to grow stronger and, therefore, you grow stronger in our Lord and to Him. He loves you so very much.

The surgeon explained the surgery to Ana Maria, telling her that he would use a scope to enter through her nasal passage and pull the tumour out through her nose, therefore, not having to make any incisions on her face. This did give Ana Maria a great relief. Not that Ana Maria is vain at all about her looks but, who would want incision scars on their face if they do not need to?

Friday morning, Ana Maria is rolled into the OR and the surgery begins. Everything goes smoothly and she is back in her room by late afternoon, still groggy from the medications. The surgeon comes into Ana Maria's room to explain how the surgery went. It was fairly successful and the surgeon was able to remove 98% of the tumour, however, a small piece had to be left behind because it was attached to a major artery and the chance of nicking the artery and Ana Maria bleeding out was too great. For that reason, that little piece of tumour was still there. Ana Maria would need to undergo 20 radiation treatments in order to hopefully shrink all that was left of the tumour. Then, she would have to take medication to help balance out her hormones. It is an imbalance in Ana Maria's hormones that caused the tumour to grow in the first place. If the hormones are not balanced out, then there are very high odds that another tumour will grow. Overall, it was pretty good news.

We were invited to share at a church in the Charleston area in July. As much as we wish that Ana Maria could have returned home by then, we were thrilled that she was still in Charleston. We were able to spend a few days with Ana Maria, which was such a blessing. We were also able to meet many of the wonderful people that God had been using to help Ana Maria.

Through various contacts, many people working hard to get medications, staff, time at the hospital, etc. donated, Ana Maria was able to complete all 20 radiation treatments in five weeks, at the end of October. The main medication that Ana Maria needs to take for the next number of years is very costly. It is a single injection, to be given once a month, at a cost of $6000USD per injection. An astronomical price. Ana Maria's endocrinologist suggested an application be made to the drug company to see if they would donate the medication. The doctor said that he would write whatever letter necessary to the drug company to help support such an application. Application was made and the drug company agreed to donate twelve months of the medication. Praise God!

After five months in Charleston, Ana Maria was ready, physically and emotionally, to return home to the Dominican Republic. We were back in the Dominican Republic and thrilled to pick her up at the airport, with her children, as she returned home. She walked out of that airport so happy and healthy. She still had a way to go as far as recovery went, but she was home.

It has now been almost two years since the surgery. Ana Maria's hormone levels are still not stabilized. She has her ups and downs as far as how she feels and how the hormone levels go. We had to switch her medication after the first year because we could no longer get the injections that she needs. We were able to switch her to a pill, which is more affordable. The only down side is that she has to take the pill every fourth day. A church back in the US has been buying the medication for Ana Maria during this second year of recovery and have committed to continue to purchase it for Ana Maria as long as they can. The endocrinologist estimates that she will need to remain on the medication for three to five years.

We all praise God, alongside of Ana Maria, for her treatments and healing and that she is healthy to raise her children. Not all days are easy for Ana Maria as she raises her children, a widow who has some health issues. However, most days are good days now as far as her health goes. She is back to work with ministry, working harder and doing more than ever before. AND - she is here for all her children, son in law and grandson.

December 2011

Excerpt from Our Newsletters

The enemy does like to attack

Two weeks after we arrived in Canada, we received an email from the landlord of the clinic asking us to move by October 31st. After almost ten years of renting this building, we were shocked by this request. The landlord has given no reason but we believe it is very spiritual; for various reasons. We contacted our Dominican lawyer to check what the laws say and learned that the landlord has to give us six months' notice, in writing, notarized and delivered by the bailiff. We emailed this information to the landlord and also asked him to consider waiting until August 31, 2012 as we are out of country. The landlord said that he will give the six months' written notice and will get that delivered to our lawyer. As of the writing of this, the landlord has yet to deliver any written notice. Prayers for the landlord to wait until we return to the DR would be appreciated.

August 2012

Excerpt from Our Newsletters

NATURAL DISASTERS

On 5 August at 2:40am, we were woken by a 4.3 earthquake. It shook the house and the sound of the rumbling ground was an amazing sound. We later discovered some serious cracks in our house from the quake. The more serious cracks go right through the entire brick walls. Paul was able to talk to an architect in Calgary and an engineer in California and they both assured us that our house responded as it should in an earthquake and there is no structural damage. Praise God! The major cracks are below and above windows and doors with no cracks in any columns.

As I write this, Paul and Daniel are at the clinic getting it prepared for Tropical Storm/Hurricane Isaac. Isaac is currently a tropical storm but is expected to be a hurricane by the time it reaches us late tonight, early tomorrow. Later this afternoon, we will prepare the house, however, the clinic is our greatest concern. The clinic is located below the road level and if there is more than two inches of water coming down the road, it will go over the gate line and pour into the clinic, flooding the clinic. We will be doing a lot of working packing of most of the clinic into plastic totes. Our greatest concern is our 12,000+ patient files and finding a way to protect them if the clinic does flood. Even if Isaac remains a tropical storm, this just means less wind but it will still bring a lot of rain and flooding does more damage than the winds.

Your prayers are greatly appreciated as we wait for Isaac to arrive.

October 2012

Excerpt from Our Newsletters

About two weeks ago, two young American missionaries (Beth and Joan) who had been here for about six months working with another ministry were brought to our clinic with flu like symptoms late in the afternoon. Dra. Wendy and I were both suspecting typhoid or Dengue so we sent them for some lab work. They were to bring the results back to us the next day so that we could determine course of treatment based on the lab work. The next morning, I, Sharyn, received a frantic call from a friend, Rachel, who has been a missionary here for over six years and supervisor to the two missionaries brought to our clinic. Rachel cries into the phone, "Sharyn, Beth is in her bed, cold and not breathing. Help". I told Rachel to wrap up Beth and take her to clinic hospital in town (owned by Dominican Christian friends). Dr. Abad has a full hospital.

I told the kids that we had an emergency, to stop school, and get ready as we have to run to town. When we arrived at Abad's clinic, Rachel, her director, and a couple other staff where outside the ER. Rachel saw me, shook her head no and wrapped her arms around me. Beth was gone. Words can not explain how much this pulled the rug out from under me and I can never explain how Rachel and the other missionary staff at this ministry felt.

We later learned that Beth had passed away four to five hours before she was found in her bed. We also learned that Beth suffered from a rare, terminal immune deficiency disease that she had not told anyone here about. Her ministry did not know about it and Beth had not told me about it the day before when I took her history. Four years ago, the specialists in the USA gave Beth about five years to live. Beth was 29 years old. Beth's death has rocked the entire Body of Christ community here and it really affected us a lot. I, especially, still feel affected from this.

The director of the ministry Beth was serving with, is fairly new here (about a year). Sometimes it takes a new person to start up what we should have been doing all along. Scott emailed a few people that he knew in the missionary community here explaining that their ministry has been feeling under attack for a few months and asking if anyone was interested in getting together for a time of joint prayer. When Scott asked us, I asked if I could pass the word around the Dominican pastor's community and his response was "invite everyone!". Scott offered lunch and then prayer from 1 - 2 pm. From Scott's first email to the prayer meeting was three days. In my guess, about 60+ people attended with about 40% of them being Dominican pastors and church leaders! It was so incredible to have this time of joint prayer together with other missionaries from different ministries and countries, other Christians, Dominican pastors........ The Body of Christ!

We had a mission team here at the time and asked the team if they would like to attend. We received a resounding YES. We stopped our work projects at noon and headed to the meeting.

We returned to work at about 2:30pm feeling the total presence of God, His power, His love and the defeat of the enemy. God promises that when more than two are gathered, their prayers are heard. The Body of Christ coming together under one roof, at the same time, is an incredible tool against the enemy. We hope and pray that this will not be the last joint prayer meeting in our area!

"He is not the God of the dead, by of the living, for to him all are alive."

Luke 20:38

November 2012

Excerpt from Our Newsletters

SO MANY CHANGES

Since stepping off the plane on 31 July in Santiago, DR, so much has happened. August was an onslaught of work, emotions, adjustments and getting back into a new normal for our family. From the moment we stepped off the plane, all our friends warned us of an increase in violent crime. So much was said in front of the kids that they still do not feel safe. Having an armed robbery, with fatalities, just 300 metres from our house did not help. We are thankful that God does protect!!! August also brought us a 5.5 earthquake which shook our house and left some major cracks in our walls. We endured the edge of Hurricane Sandy with four days of solid rain, some flooding but nothing compared to the US Eastern coast.

Samantha adjusted back to life here the quickest. She has gotten back in with all her friends, and decided to take on soccer this year rather than ballet. Noah has not made friends yet but is enjoying soccer three times a week. Both kids love to skype with friends back in Three Hills and do that quite regularly. The kids are doing well with their home school, working hard and advancing through the school year with good grades.

March 2013

Excerpt from Our Newsletters

Vangela and Domingo are a sweet, older couple. Vangela cleans someone's home for about five hours a day while Domingo sits out in his yard, at his very old sewing machine, sewing various items for his trait as a tailor. In 2005, they applied to our ministry for help to build a better house. This couple has three children. One of their daughter's died in an auto accident about six year ago. Their son and other daughter live with their spouses in Santo Domingo so they do not get to see them more than about once a year, if that. They have been living in a falling down, wooden shack. In 2006, we built some of the walls in block, around the wooden house but were never able to complete the job. In February, Trochu Baptist Church from Trochu, Alberta, sent down a team of fifteen who tackled this house. By the time that they left, all the walls were completed, the header done, the roof on, walls plastered and the electrical laid out. All that is left to make it liveable is a floor, door, windows and to complete the electrical. Vangela and Domingo are so happy and thrilled. They could not stop praising God when the team made their final rounds to pray with the families that they helped.

We have a team from Victoria arriving in just a few days. One of the many projects for this team will be to pour the floor and complete the electrical for Domingo and Vangela.

The Trochu team was with us for twelve days and they accomplished so much! On the practical side, they not only did Domingo and Vangela's home, they completed Cristina's house with plastering, painting, electrical and plumbing. They poured a couple columns at Nena's house, painted the clinic and spent a week working on a local church. At the church, they built a platform, a railing around the stage, lots of electrical and built a Sunday school room out the back of the church. Such a blessing to this church that blesses all those around them in a poor neighbourhood of town. This team also brought down 200 pairs of new shoes that were donated. These shoes were distributed to Pedregal, the church we worked with and also some were sent to a church in Haiti that our local church helps to support. On the spiritual side, many hearts were touched and came closer to God. Those around the church have been questioning the pastor and church leadership about why the "gringos" were working there and it has opened many doors to evangelize. Paul and Daniel have also had some doors open to some people in Pedregal who are now asking questions about our Lord and God. Amen!

Clinic Turns 10 years' old

Excerpt from Our Newsletters

23 February 2012 marked the 10th anniversary of our medical clinic. It is hard to believe that it has been ten years. We did some calculations that you might find interesting. In these ten years:

- 15 local doctors have volunteered month and/or years to serve at the clinic
- we now have two full time and one half time paid staff
- we have seen over 13,000 patients
- we have moved from paper to computer files
- we have no idea how many people have accepted the Lord but it has been many.

God is so good and faithful. We give all the glory to HIM. On Saturday 2 March, we had a nice, intimate celebration of the ten years with some words and prayers shared..... and cake, of course.

April 2013

Excerpt from Our Newsletters

GOD'S LOVE AND MESSAGE IS BEING SHARED!

Every Wednesday afternoon, the Dominican ladies in the little church close to where our clinic is located, go out "visiting". This small group of evangelical ladies only purpose is to bring people closer to Jesus Christ. In the village, there are about 2300 people, very densely populated. The ladies go to a different area of the village each Wednesday afternoon. They are so faithful and they never miss a Wednesday. Sometimes, one of the ladies may not be there due to illness or something but there is always a group that goes. They meet up at the clinic at 3 pm and head out to share God's love and Word. I find this little group of ladies so encouraging and I have personally witnessed the fruits of their obedience to God. Hearts have changed and continue to change towards God all the time - thanks to this faithful group of God's apostles. May we all be more like these ladies.

August 2013

Excerpt from Our Newsletters

"No one has come to teach us these things. It is such an amazing thing of God that He sent these people to teach us." This is just one of many quotes that pastors and church leaders shared with us at the end of the Pastors' Conference that we hosted in mid-July. Two couples from New Covenant Life Ministry Church in New Jersey dedicated a week to come to Jarabacoa to teach local pastors and church leaders about finances and "Character and Integrity in the Church". The presence of God was there for every workshop. About 100 different pastors and church leaders attended part or all of the three day conference. After the first workshop, our local pastor was calling every member of our church and telling them they had to attend. Dominican pastors and church leaders do not get opportunities to receive teachings and it was awesome to see God bring this about.

December 2013

Excerpt from Our Newsletters

WITNESSING GOD

Sometimes, we see God move in mighty ways that takes your breath away. Other times, it is a slow progression. Many of you know our Dominican foster daughter, Anny. Anny lived with us during the week while attending school then with her Grandma on the weekends for about seven years. As any parent does, you pray that your children will choose to follow God. Last November, Anny ran away when she discovered that she was pregnant. It has been a tough year as Anny has been forced to grow up quickly. She had to drop out of school and chose to move in with Anthony. After many difficult months, Anny and Anthony decided to follow God and make God the head of their home. In June, they legally married. In July, Nashley was born. Anny and Anthony are active members of their church, started a Bible study in their apartment building and are growing a strong family of God. Before we came to Canada in November, Anny told me that she remembers all the things that we have taught her and is so happy to be living her life for God. Praise God for Anny, Antoni and Nashley as they live for God.

"As the body without spirit is dead, so faith without deeds is dead."

James 2:26

2014

Noé

When Noé was little, his father left his mother and Noé did not see his father again. After a while, Noé's mother remarried and had three more children with Noé's stepfather. Noé's stepfather never treated him like his own children. Noé was treated like an outcast and never felt loved. By the time that Noé was 19 years old, he was very depressed. One evening, he was seriously thinking about taking his own life. It was this evening that Noé felt God speaking to him and telling him to go to church. The feeling was so strong that Noé did go to church. At church, he met some nice people who treated him with love and told him about God. It was through this church that Noé learned about God, felt loved and accepted. Noé turned to God, giving his life to God.

Noé had a job, was attending church, making new friends and a new church family. One evening, Noé has a dream. In this dream, Noé met a young lady and they became friends. It was a nice dream but Noé did not think much more about it. A couple months later, while at church, a man in the church invited Noé over to his house and told him there was someone that Noé had to meet. Noé went to this man's house and when he arrived, a young lady came out of the house. It was the same young lady that he saw in his dream. When Noé met Anna, he felt something weird inside of him. Something special but something that he had never felt before. He felt like he had known Anna his entire life, although he just met her. When he was not with Anna, he could not think of anything except for Anna. Every time they parted, Noé could not wait until the next that he would be able to see Anna. About a year later, Noé and Anna married.

Now that they were married, they, like most of us, wanted a house. In the DR, people will build their houses on family property. As Noé and Ana's families are poor, there was not a lot of options. Noé's mom said that Noé could build his house on top of her house. She had a concrete roof and a second floor could be built. Noé was working hard and saving all his money, to buy some bricks and a bag of concrete. Over time, Noé and Ana's house was starting to come together, and, they now had two small children. Then Noé's half-brother was diagnosed with cancer. There is no medical insurance in the DR so people have to pay for all doctor consults, tests, medications, treatments, etc. The family started to borrow and sell items in order to pay for the half-brother's medical care. Noé's mother took out loans, using her house a collateral. Noé's half-brother passed away and the family could not pay the creditors. The creditors took the house and just like that, Noé and Ana were homeless. Noé came home from work to find his wife, two children, their mattress and clothing on the street and they had nowhere to go.

Noé worked hard and was able to rent a very small house made out of wood and, literally, leaning over and falling down. Noé and Ana were praying for a house of their own. Noé was able to get a very small piece of land that is approximately 15' x

30'. However, they do not have the ability to get any building materials to build a house.

It is 2013 when Noé wakes up from a very vivid dream. Noé dreamt that God was speaking to him and telling him that in 2015, he would be given the keys to his own house. Noé believed God but was not sure if it was a dream and promise from God or not. About two months later, a girl from church comes to Noé and Ana to tell them about a dream that she had. She told them that she had the dream two days earlier and feels that God is not letting her forget about it until she shares it with Noé and Ana. She then proceeds to tell Noé and Ana that God said in her dream that in 2015, the keys to their own house would be handed to them. This all took place in 2013.

In September 2014, House Upon the Rock Ministry decided that the next house project that we would take on would be for a family in the village who were living in a rented, wood house that was falling down and were in desperate need of a house. In October 2014, the first team began work on this house. The couple owned a very small piece of land but had no means to buy building materials. It is the house of Noé and Ana. A second team continued on the house in November, a third and fourth team continued work on Noé and Ana's house in March 2015.

While the March teams were working on Noé and Ana's house, Paul asked Noé to share his testimony with the teams. Paul had heard a little of Noé's testimony but had not heard the entire testimony. Paul had heard bits of Noé's testimony over the past several months as Noé shared stories of his life with Paul while they worked on his. I had never Noé's testimony and now I was translating it for one of the teams. When Noé finished telling the team his story, there was not a dry eye among us, including myself.

As of Easter Friday, Noé's house nearly completed. The floors are now done, the windows and doors are being installed, some of the electrical and plumbing is also completed. We are hoping to hand over the keys to Noé and Ana to their new home within the next week or two.

In April 2015, God's promise came true as we handed Noé and Ana keys to their new house. It is not a huge house but it is a strong, safe house. It is a house dedicated to God and is now home for Noé, Ana and their two children.

At the time that Paul and our Dominican Board selected Noé and Ana as our next house to build, none of us had any idea about the prophetic words that God had given Noé through the two dreams back in 2013. We did not know about this until the middle of March 2015 and, by that time, it was already clear that Noé, Ana and their children would be living in their new house in 2015.

Praise God for this new house for Noé and Ana, for all the teams that have been a huge part of building the house and providing funds to buy construction materials, for God and His faithfulness and His blessings to His children in such special ways that can only be God.

December 2014

Excerpt from Our Newsletters

IMPACT OF TEAMS

People often ask us how a mission team can evangelize when they do not speak the language? When a mission team comes, they are a living testimony to what God calls us all to do. Go! Team members have paid their own money, putting hours of fund raising, used up vacation time, left behind family to hold down the home front, taken leave from school knowing the hard work needed to catch up on missed assignments to go on a mission trip. They come to serve, to help and be a light of God. The local people often ask us what we are paying the teams to work. When we explain that we have paid nothing and the team has paid everything, the people are shocked. This opens the door to explaining WHY the teams sacrifice so much to come to the heat, sweating to build someone's house that they do not even know. We may be the voice talking to the local people to share the Word of God but the team members are sharing the Acts of God. Without the teams, the doors would not be open to share about God with the local people. Through our November teams, five people asked Jesus into their lives and now are living their lives for God. PRAISE GOD!!!!

December 2015

Excerpt from Our Newsletters

SIMPLE PRAYERS ANSWERED

The other day started with so many little problems. By 10 am, we were all feeling very attacked by the enemy. Our local construction professional woke up sick and could not work. This left Paul without Tony to finish up the door frames and windows on the new house. This needed to be completed by Wednesday when the doors and windows were being installed. As we turned on the clinic computers, the secretary and doctor's computers would not allow us to log into our clinic program where we have all our patient files. Monday are our busiest day and, by 9:30 am, we had 15 people waiting with things slowed to a crawl due to the computer problems. We could not figure out how to fix it. We had someone seek Paul and I out to ask for help for her family who are in crisis and in need of help and counselling. One of our staff, who was in charge of one of our ministry construction sites, had to leave suddenly for a family emergency and take his wife to the hospital immediately. All this and it was not even 10 am. Paul, Mike and I stopped to pray. Mike asked God to give someone an idea to fix the computers, just a simple, quick fix idea that would work. We lifted up the issues as well. Then I prayed with Wendy and Juana (doctor and secretary). About two minutes later, an idea popped into my head.

I went to Wendy's computer and tried it - it worked! I opened the clinic program and Wendy could start using it to consult with patients. I went to Juana's computer to try the same thing and, it worked! Juana could now register the patients. It seems small and simple but it was a true and instant answer to prayer. An answer that made the entire day at the clinic flow smoother. As the morning went on, the other issues were also solved. God does hear all our prayers. He does not always answer them as we want or when we want, but He does hear each and every one of them! Never stop praying.

2015

TESTIMONY & LESSONS FOR US –
Excerpt from Our Newsletters

In the first week of December, we must finish the house that we are building. The family that the house is for has been told that they have to move out of the wood, falling down shack that they rent by December 6th and they have nowhere to go. It will be tight but, thanks be to God and to six mission teams, we will get this family into their new house by the 6th. A few things will still need to be completed (like the kitchen), but they will have a house to move into. This is one of the poorest families that we have ever built a house for but you would never know it if you met this family. They are so grateful to God for their lives, they never ask for anything, they do not advertise when have no food to eat or only enough food for their kids and none for the parents. After knowing this family for about six years, just last month we found out that they go days without food on a very regular basis. We had no idea! This family just keeps on praising God. They have been a real testimony to us as they have so much less than any one of us yet they do not complain, do not "poor talk", they just keep praising God. We are so honoured that God chose House Upon the Rock Ministry to be a part of blessing this family with a new house that is all theirs! Now their rent money can go towards food for their family.

"Then Jesus cam to them and said, All authority in heaven and on earth has been given to me. Therefore go and make disciples of all nations, baptizing them in the name of the Father and of the Son and of the Holy Spirit and teaching them to obey everything I have commanded you. And surely I will be with you always, to the very end of the age."

Matthew 28:18-20

Epilogue

God's Stories are not over. From when I started to write this book until I finished, I added a few more stories because God never ends. His stories are never over. There is not a last page to God's Stories. As you finish this book, my prayer is that it has brought some inspiration and encouragement to your personal relationship God. I hear so often in today's day and age that the miracles that we read in the Bible do not happen anymore. I pray that this book reminds us that God is the same yesterday, today and tomorrow. Would God not still be performing the same miracles today? I know that He is! Do you?